Life in the UK

Second Editic.

Study Guide
And
Multiple Choice Practice Questions

Study Guide containing chapters 2, 3, 4, 5 and 6 of the Life in the United Kingdom: Journey to Citizenship handbook and 700 practice questions

Published by Teranet Ltd

Teranet Ltd
Sussex Innovation Centre
Science Park Square
Falmer
BN1 9SB

First published in Great Britain 2007

ISBN 0-9553899-1-7

ISBN 978-0-9553899-1-7

CONTENTS

Introduction

This book is a study guide for those candidates intending to take the 'Citizenship Test' to become a British citizen or to get settlement visa.

The British government has recently introduced a theoretical test to ensure that, those who apply for British citizenship have some knowledge of English and familiarity with life in the United Kingdom. A guidebook entitled 'Life in the UK' was published by the HMSO to give basic information that every citizen should know. Chapters 2, 3, 4, 5 and 6 of this guide are reproduced in this study guide for the candidates to learn, what we feel crucial to the Life in the UK test.

The citizenship practice tests given in this book are questions designed to test the knowledge acquired from reading the material in the guide. There are some additional questions to practice on other aspects of life in the UK. Candidates must read the material given and test themselves with the practice questions until they have confidence to answer questions without referring to the material.

These sample questions are intended for the candidates to practice and gain confidence before taking the citizenship test. The questions asked at the citizenship test will not be exactly the same as given in this guide.

Our website www.britishness-test.co.uk is regularly updated to reflect changes in the material provided. Check our website for the latest updates to the material and practice tests.

Preface

How to use this handbook

This handbook is intended for those readers who are intending to become permanent residents or citizens of the United Kingdom, and are studying it in order to take the tests of knowledge of English and of life in the United Kingdom which all applicants now need to pass.

Since 2005, everyone who applies to become a British citizen has had to show their knowledge of the English language and of life in the United Kingdom in one of two ways. They can take a special ESOL (English for Speakers of Other Languages) course, which uses teaching materials based on the practical meaning of citizenship. Or they can take the new Life in the UK test, which consists of 24 questions about important aspects of life in Britain today. Those 24 questions will be different for each person taking the test. The Life in the UK Test will normally be taken in English, although special arrangements can be made if anyone wishes to take it in Welsh or Scottish Gaelic. The questions are deliberately written in a way that requires an understanding of the English language at the level (called ESOL Entry 3 level) that the law requires of people becoming British citizens. So there is no need to take a separate test of knowledge of the English language.

From 2 April 2007, everyone who applies for permanent residence in the United Kingdom (often called 'settlement' or 'indefinite leave to remain') will also need to qualify either by taking the special ESOL course or by passing the Life in the UK test. A person who qualifies for settlement in either of these ways will not need to go through the same process again if he or she later decides to apply for British citizenship. This handbook contains all the answers to the questions that may be asked in the Life in the UK test. The questions will all be based on chapters 2,3,4,5 and 6 of the handbook. You do not have to study the other chapters in order to be able to pass the test. The handbook has been written to ensure that anyone who can read English at the ESOL Entry 3 level or above should have no difficulty with the language.

To provide extra help for readers who are not native English speakers, we have provided at the end of the handbook a glossary of some key words and phrases, which you may find helpful. We have also highlighted some areas that are particularly important. These are headed 'Make sure you understand' but are intended only as guidance; reading just these sections will not enough to pass the test. You may not get questions on these highlighted areas, and you may be asked about topics that have not been highlighted. So please make sure you read each chapter carefully.

If you want to find out more information about the Life in the UK test, please visit the website of UFI, the company that manages them on behalf of the Home Office. This website (www.lifeintheuktest.gov.uk) gives contact details for centres where the test can be taken, background information about the tests and the fees involved, and also offers a sample test to give you an idea of what to expect. If you want information about the alternative way of obtaining permanent residence by taking a special ESOL with citizenship course, the UFI helpline on 0800 0154245, and your local library, are good sources of information on colleges offering these courses in your area.

The Government welcomes new migrants to Britain. We very much hope that those who meet our residence qualifications and decide to spend their lives in this country will seek permanent settlement, and will eventually go on to become British citizens.

A CHANGING SOCIETY

In this chapter there is information about:

Migration to Britain

- The long history of immigration to the United Kingdom
- Different reasons why people migrated to the UK
- Basic changes in immigration patterns over the last 30 years

The changing role of women

- Changes to family structures and women's rights since the 19th century
- Women's campaigns for rights, including the right to vote, in the late 19th and early 20th centuries
- Discrimination against women in the workplace and in education
- Changing attitudes to women working, and responsibilities of men and women in the home

Children, family and young people

- The identity, interests, tastes and lifestyle patterns of children and young people
- Education and work
- Health hazards: cigarettes, alcohol and illegal drugs
- Young people's political and social attitudes

Migration to Britain

Many people living in Britain today have their origins in other countries. They can trace their roots to regions throughout the world such as Europe, the Middle East, Africa, Asia and the Caribbean. In the distant past, invaders came to Britain, seized land and stayed. More recently, people come to Britain to find safety, jobs and a better life.

Britain is proud of its tradition of offering safety to people who are escaping persecution and hardship. For example, in the 16th and 18th centuries, Huguenots (French Protestants) came to Britain to escape religious persecution in France. In the mid - 1840s there was a terrible famine in Ireland and many Irish people migrated to Britain. Many Irish men became labourers and helped to build canals and railways across Britain.

From 1880 to 1910, a large number of Jewish people came to Britain to escape racist attacks (called 'pogroms') in what was then called the Russian Empire and from the countries now called Poland, Ukraine and Belarus.

Migration since 1945

After the Second World War (1939-45), there was a huge task of rebuilding Britain. There were not enough people to do the work, so the British government encouraged workers from Ireland and other parts of Europe to come to the UK to help with the reconstruction. In 1948, people from the West Indies were also invited to come and work.

During the 1950s, there was still a shortage of labour in the UK. The UK encouraged immigration in the 1950s for economic reasons and many industries advertised for workers from overseas. For example, centres were set up in the West Indies to recruit people to drive buses. Textile and engineering firms from the north of England and the Midlands sent agents to India and Pakistan to find workers. For about 25 years, people from the West Indies, India, Pakistan, and later Bangladesh, travelled to work and settle in Britain.

The number of people migrating from these areas fell in the late 1960s because the government passed new laws to restrict immigration to Britain, although immigrants from 'old' Commonwealth countries such as Australia, New Zealand and Canada did not have to face such strict controls. During this time, however, Britain did admit 28,000 people of Indian origin who had been forced to leave Uganda and 22,000 refugees from South East Asia.

In the 1980s the largest immigrant groups came from the United States, Australia, South Africa and New Zealand. In the early 1990s, groups of people from the former Soviet Union came to Britain looking for a new and safer way of life. Since 1994 there has been a global rise in mass migration for both political and economic reasons.

Check that you understand:

- Some of the historical reasons for immigration to the UK
- Some of the reasons for immigration to the UK since 1945
- The main immigrant groups coming to the UK since 1945, the countries they came from and kind of work they did.

The changing role of women

In 19th-century Britain, families were usually large and in many poorer homes men, women and children all contributed towards the family income. Although they made an important economic contribution, women in Britain had fewer rights than men. Until 1857, a married woman had no right to divorce her husband. Until 1882, when a woman got married, her earnings, property and money automatically belonged to her husband.

In the late 19th and early 20th centuries, an increasing number of women campaigned and demonstrated for greater rights and, in particular, the right to vote. They became known as 'Suffragettes'. These protests decreased during the First World War because women joined in the war effort and therefore did a much greater variety of work than they had before. When the First World War ended in 1918, women over the age of 30 were finally given the right to vote and to stand for election to Parliament. It was not until 1928 that women won the right to vote at 21, at the same age as men.

Despite these improvements, women still faced discrimination in the workplace. For example, it was quite common for employers to ask women to leave their jobs when they got married. Many jobs were closed to women and it was difficult for women to enter universities. During the 1960s and 1970s there was increasing pressure from women for equal rights. Parliament passed new laws giving women the right to equal pay and prohibiting employers from discriminating against women because of their sex.

Women in Britain today

Women in Britain today make up 51% of the population and 45% of the workforce. These days girls leave school, on average, with better qualifications than the boys and there are now more women than men at university.

Employment opportunities for women are now much greater than they were in the past. Although women continue to be employed in traditional female areas such as healthcare, teaching, secretarial and retail work, there is strong evidence that attitudes are changing, and women are now active in a much wider range of work than before. Research shows that very few people today believe that women in Britain should stay at home and not go out to work. Today, almost three-quarters of women with school-age children are in paid work.

In most households, women continue to have the main responsibility for childcare and housework. There is evidence that there is now greater equality in homes and that more men are taking some responsibility for raising the family and doing housework. Despite this progress, many people believe that more needs to be done to achieve greater equality for women. There are still examples of discrimination against women, particularly in the workplace, despite the laws that exist to prevent it. Women still do not always have the same access to promotion and better-paid jobs. The average hourly pay rate for women is 20% less than for men and after leaving university most women still earns less than men.

Check that you understand:

- When women aged over 30 were first given the right to vote
- When women were given equal voting rights with men
- Some of the important developments to create equal rights in the workplace.

Children, family and young people

In the UK, there are almost 15 million children and young people up to the age of 19. This is almost one-quarter of the UK population.

Over the last 20 years, family patterns in Britain have been transformed because of changing attitudes towards divorce and separation. Today, 65% of children live with birth parents, almost 25% live in lone-parent families, and 10% live within a stepfamily. Most children in Britain receive weekly pocket money from their parents and many get extra money for doing jobs around the house.

Children in the UK do not play outside the home as much as they did in the past. Part of the reason for this is increased home entertainment such as television, videos and computers. There is also increased concern for children's safety and there are many stories in newspapers about child molestation by strangers, but there is no evidence that this kind of danger is increasing.

Young people have different identities, interests and fashions to older people. Many young people move away from their family home when they become adults but this varies from one community to another.

Education

The law states that children between the ages of 5 and 16 must attend school. The tests that pupils take are very important, and in England and Scotland

7

children take national tests in English, mathematics and science when they are 7, 11 and 14 years old. (In Wales, teachers assess children's progress when they are 7 and 11 and they take a national test at the age of 14). The tests give important information about children's progress and achievement, the subjects they are doing well in and the areas where they need extra help.

Most young people take the General Certificate of Secondary Education (GCSE), or, in Scotland, Scottish Qualifications Authority (SQA) Standard Grade examinations when they are 16. At 17 and 18, many take vocational qualifications, General Certificates of Education at an Advanced level (AGCEs), AS level units or Higher/Advanced Higher Grades in Scotland. Schools and colleges will expect good GCSE or SQA Standard Grade results before allowing a student to enrol on an AGCE or Scottish Higher/Advanced Higher course.

AS levels are Advanced Subsidiary qualifications gained by completing three AS units. Three AS units are considered as one-half of an AGCE. In the second part of the course, three more AS units can be studied to complete the AGCE qualification.

Many people refer to AGCEs by the old name of A levels. AGCEs are the traditional route for entry to higher education courses, but many higher education students enter with different kinds of qualifications.

One in three young people now go on to higher education at college or university. Some young people defer their university entrance for a year and take a 'gap year'. This year out of education often includes voluntary work and travel overseas. Some young people work to earn and save money to pay for their university fees and living expenses.

People over 16 years of age may also choose to study at Colleges of Further Education or Adult Education Centres. There is a wide range of academic and vocational courses available as well as courses which develop leisure interests and skills. Contact your local college for details.

Work

It is common for young people to have a part-time job while they are still at school. It is thought there are 2 million children at work at any one time. The most common jobs are newspaper delivery and work in supermarkets and newsagents. Many parents believe that part-time work helps children to become more independent as well as providing them (and sometimes their families) with extra income.

There are laws about the age when children can take up paid work (usually not before 14), the type of work they can do and the number of hours they can work (see www.worksmart.org.uk for more information).

It is very important to note that there are concerns for the safety of children who work illegally or who are not properly supervised and the employment of children is strictly controlled by law.

Health hazards

Many parents worry that their children may misuse drugs and addictive substances.

Smoking:

Although cigarette smoking has fallen in the adult population, more young people are smoking, and more girls smoke than boys. By law, it is illegal to sell tobacco products to anyone under 16 years old. In some areas, smoking in public buildings and work environments is not allowed.

Alcohol:

Young people under the age of 18 are not allowed to buy alcohol in Britain, but there is concern about the age some young people start drinking alcohol and the amount of alcohol they drink at one time, known as 'binge drinking'. It is illegal to be drunk in public and there are now more penalties to help control this problem, including on-the-spot fines.

Illegal drugs:

As in most countries, it is illegal to possess drugs such as heroin, cocaine, ecstasy, amphetamines and cannabis. Current statistics show that half of all young adults, and about a third of the population as a whole, have used illegal drugs at one time or another.

There is a strong link between the use of hard drugs (e.g. crack cocaine and heroin) and crime, and also hard drugs and mental illness. The misuse of drugs has a huge social and financial cost for the country. This is a serious issue and British society needs to find an effective way of dealing with the problem.

Young people's political and social attitudes

Young people in Britain can vote in elections from the age of 18. In the 2001 general election, however, only 1 in 5 first-time voters used their vote. There has been a great debate over the reasons for this. Some researchers think that one reason is that young people are not interested in the political process.

Although most young people show little interest in party politics, there is strong evidence that many are interested in specific political issues such as the environment and cruelty to animals.

In 2003 a survey of young people in England and Wales showed that they believe the five most important issues in Britain were crime, drugs, war/ terrorism, racism and health. The same survey asked young people about their participation in political and community events. They found that 86% of young people had taken part in some form of community event over the past year, and 50% had taken part in fund-raising or collecting money for charity. Similar results have been found in surveys in Scotland and Northern Ireland. Many children first get involved in these activities while at school where they study Citizenship as part of the National Curriculum.

Check that you understand the key terms and vocabulary for this chapter

Migration to Britain:

    migrate, immigrate, immigration, immigrant
    persecution, famine, conflict
    labour, labourer
    recruit
    restrict
    political asylum
    the war effort

Changing role of women:

    income, earnings
    rights, equal rights
    campaign, demonstrate
    discriminate, discrimination
    prohibit
    workforce
    household
    promotion

Children, family and young people:

    eligible
    concern
    molestation
    attitudes
    hazards

birth parent, stepfamily
compulsory
informal
methods of assessment
defer
gap year
independent
income
misuse
addictive substances
abuse
binge drinking
on-the-spot fines
controlled drugs
criminal offence
possess
heroin, cocaine, crack cocaine, ecstasy, amphetamines, cannabis
burglary, mugging
debate
politicians, political process, party politics, political issues
specific
concern
environment
terrorism, racism
participation
fund-raising

UK TODAY: A PROFILE

In this chapter there is information about:

- The population of the UK
- The census
- Ethnic diversity
- The regions of Britain
- Religion and religious freedom
- Customs and traditions

Population

In 2005 the population of the United Kingdom was just under 60 million people.

UK population 2005

England	(84% of the population)	50.1 million
Scotland	(8% of the population)	5.1 million
Wales	(5% of the population)	2.9 million
N. Ireland	(3% of the population)	1.7 million
Total UK		59.8 million

Source: National Statistics

The population has grown by 7.7% since 1971, and growth has been faster in more recent years. Although the general population in the UK has increased in the last 20 years, in some areas such as the North-East and North-West of England there has been a decline.

Both the birth rate and the death rate are falling and as a result the UK now has an ageing population. For instance, there are more people over 60 than children under 16. There are also a record number of people aged 85 and over.

The census

A census is a count of the whole population. It also collects statistics on topics such as age, place of birth, occupation, ethnicity, housing, health, and marital status.

A census has been taken every ten years since 1801, except during the Second World War. The next census will take place in 2011.

During a census, a form is delivered to every household in the country. This form asks for detailed information about each member of the household and must be completed by law. The information remains confidential and anonymous; it can only be released to the public after 100 years, when many people researching their family history find it very useful. General census information is used to identify population trends and to help planning. More information about the census, the census form and statistics from previous censuses can be found at www.statistics.gov.uk/census.

Ethnic diversity

The UK population is ethnically diverse and is changing rapidly, especially in large cities such as London, so it is not always easy to get an exact picture of the ethnic origin of all the population from census statistics. Each of the four countries of the UK (England, Wales, Scotland and Northern Ireland) has different customs, attitudes and histories.

People of Indian, Pakistani, Chinese, Black Caribbean, Black African, Bangladeshi and mixed ethnic descent make up 8.3% of the UK population. Today about half the members of these communities were born in the United Kingdom.

There are also considerable numbers of people resident in the UK who are of Irish, Italian, Greek and Turkish Cypriot, Polish, Australian, Canadian, New Zealand and American descent. Large numbers have also arrived since 2004 from the new East European member states of the European Union. These groups are not identified separately in the census statistics in the following table.

UK population 2001

	Million	UK population %
White (including people of European, Australian, American descent)	54.2	92
Mixed	0.7	1.2
Asian or Asian British		
Indian	1.1	1.8
Pakistani	0.7	1.3
Bangladeshi	0.3	0.5
Other Asian	0.2	0.4
Black or Black British		
Black Caribbean	0.6	1.0
Black African	0.5	0.8
Black other	0.1	0.2
Chinese	0.2	0.4
Other	0.2	0.4

Source: National Statistics from the 2001 census

Where do the largest ethnic minority groups live?

The figures from the 2001 census show that most members of the large ethnic minority groups in the UK live in England, where they make up 9% of the total population. 45% of all ethnic minority people live in the London area, where they form nearly one-third of the population (29%). Other areas of England with large ethnic minority populations are the West Midlands, the South East, the North West, and Yorkshire and Humberside.

Proportion of ethnic minority groups in the countries of the UK

England	9%
Scotland	2%
Wales	2%
Northern Ireland	less than 1%

The nations and regions of the UK

The UK is a medium-sized country. The longest distance on the mainland, from John O'Groats on the north coast of Scotland to Land's End in the south-west corner of England, is about 870 miles (approximately 1,400 kilometres). Most of the population live in towns and cities.

There are many variations in culture and language in the different parts of the United Kingdom. This is seen in differences in architecture, in some local customs, in types of food, and especially in language. The English language has many accents and dialects. These are a clear indication of regional differences in the UK. Well-known dialects in England are Geordie (Tyneside), Scouse (Liverpool) and Cockney (London). Many other languages in addition to English are spoken in the UK, especially in multicultural cities.

In Wales, Scotland and Northern Ireland, people speak different varieties and dialects of English. In Wales, too, an increasing number of people speak Welsh, which is taught in schools and universities. In Scotland Gaelic is spoken in some parts of the Highlands and Islands and in Northern Ireland a few people speak Irish Gaelic. Some of the dialects of English spoken in Scotland show the influence of the old Scottish language, Scots. One of the dialects spoken in Northern Ireland is called Ulster Scots.

Check that you understand:

- The size of the current UK population
- The population of Scotland, Wales and Northern Ireland
- What the census is and when the next one will be
- What the largest ethnic minorities in the UK are
- Where most ethnic minority people live
- What languages other than English are spoken in Wales, Scotland and Northern Ireland
- Some of the ways you can identify regional differences in the UK

Religion

Although the UK is historically a Christian society, everyone has the legal right to practise the religion of their choice. In the 2001 census, just over 75% said they had a religion: 7 out of 10 of these were Christians. There were also a considerable number of people who followed other religions. Although many people in the UK said they held religious beliefs, currently only around 10% of the population attend religious services. More people attend services in Scotland and Northern Ireland than in England and Wales, In London the number of people who attend religious services is increasing.

Religions in the UK	%
Christian (10% of whom are Roman Catholic)	71.6
Muslim	2.7
Hindu	1%
Sikh	0.6
Jewish	0.5
Buddhist	0.3
Other	0.3
Total All	77
No religion	15.5
Not Stated	7.3

Source: National Statistics from the 2001 census

The Christian Churches

In England there is a constitutional link between church and state. The official church of the state is the Church of England. The Church of England is called the Anglican Church in other countries and the Episcopal Church in Scotland and in the USA. The Church of England is a Protestant church and has existed since the Reformation in the 1530s. The king or queen (the monarch) is the head, or Supreme Governor, of the Church of England. The monarch is not allowed to marry anyone who is not Protestant. The spiritual leader of the Church of England is the Archbishop of Canterbury. The monarch has the right to select the Archbishop and other senior church officials, but usually the choice is made by the Prime Minister and a committee appointed by the Church. Several Church of England bishops sit in the House of Lords. In Scotland, the established church is the Presbyterian Church; its head is the Chief Moderator. There is no established church in Wales or in Northern Ireland.

Other Protestant Christian groups in the UK are Baptists, Presbyterians, Method-ists and Quakers. 10% of Christians are Roman Catholic (40% in Northern Ireland).

Patron saints

England, Scotland, Wales and Northern Ireland each have a national saint called a patron saint. Each saint has a feast day. In the past these were celebrated as holy days when many people had a day off work. Today these are not public holidays except for 17 March in Northern Ireland.

Patron saints' days

St. David's day, Wales	1 March
St. Patrick's day, Northern Ireland	17 March
St George's day, England	23 April
St. Andrew's day, Scotland	30 November

There are also four public holidays a year called Bank Holidays. These are of no religious or national significance.

Check that you understand:

- The percentage (%) of the UK population who say they are Christian
- How many people say they have no religion
- What percentage are Muslim, Hindu, Sikh, Jewish, Buddhist
- Everyone in the UK has the right to practise their religion
- The Anglican Church, or Church of England, is church of the state in England (established church)
- The monarch (king or queen) is head of the church of England
- In Scotland the established church is the Presbyterian Church of Scotland. In Wales and Northern Ireland there is no established church

Customs and Traditions

Festivals

Throughout the year there are festivals of art, music and culture, such as the Notting Hill Carnival in west London and the Edinburgh Festival. Customs and traditions from various religions, such as Eid ul-Fitr (Muslim), Diwali (Hindu) and Hanukkah (Jewish) are widely recognised in the UK. Children learn about these at school. The main Christian festivals are Christmas and Easter. There are also celebrations of non-religious traditions such as New Year.

The main Christian festivals

Christmas Day

25 December, celebrates the birth of Jesus Christ. It is a public holiday. Many Christians go to church on Christmas Eve (24 December) or on Christmas Day itself. Christmas is also usually celebrated by people who are not Christian. People usually spend the day at home and eat a special meal, which often includes turkey. They give each other gifts, send each other cards and decorate their houses. Many people decorate a tree. Christmas is a special time for children. Very young children believe that an old man, Father Christmas (or Santa Claus), brings them presents during the night. He is always shown in pictures with a long white beard, dressed in red. Boxing Day, 26 December, is the day after Christmas. It is a public holiday.

Other festivals and traditions

New Year

1 January, is a public holiday. People usually celebrate on the night of 31 December. In Scotland, 31 December is called Hogmanay and 2 January is also a public holiday. In Scotland Hogmanay is a bigger holiday for some people than Christmas.

Valentine's Day

14 February, is when lovers exchange cards and gifts. Sometimes people send anonymous cards to someone they secretly admire.

April fool's Day

1 April, is a day when people play jokes on each other until midday. Often TV and newspapers carry stories intended to deceive credulous viewers and readers.

Mother's Day

The Sunday three weeks before Easter is a day when children send cards or buy gifts for their mothers. Easter is also an important Christian festival.

18

Halloween

31 October, is a very ancient festival. Young people will often dress up in frightening costumes to play 'trick or treat'. Giving them sweets or chocolates might stop them playing a trick on you. Sometimes people carry lanterns made out of pumpkins with a candle inside.

Guy Fawkes Night

5 November, is an occasion when people in Great Britain set off fireworks at home or in special displays. The origin of this celebration was an event in 1605, when a group of Catholics led by Guy Fawkes failed in their plan to kill the Protestant king with a bomb in the Houses of Parliament.

Remembrance Day

11 November, commemorates those who died fighting in World War 1, World War 2 and other wars. Many people wear poppies (a red flower) in memory of those who died. At 11a.m. there is a two-minute silence.

Sport

Sport of all kinds plays a important part in many people's lives, Football, tennis, rugby and cricket are very popular sports in the UK. There are no United Kingdom teams for football and rugby. England, Scotland, Wales and Northern Ireland have their own teams. Important sporting events include, the Grand National horse race, the Football Association (FA) cup final (and equivalents in Northern Ireland, Scotland and Wales), the Open golf championship and the Wimbledon tennis tournament.

Check that you understand:

- Which sports are most popular in the UK
- The patron saints' days in England, Scotland, Wales and Northern Ireland
- What Bank Holidays are
- The main traditional festivals in the UK
- That the main festivals in the UK are Christian based, but that important festivals from other religions are recognised and explained to children in schools

---

HOW THE UNITED KINGDOM IS GOVERNED

In this chapter there is information about:

Government

- The system of government
- The monarchy
- The electoral system
- Political parties
- Being a citizen
- Voting
- Contacting your MP
- The UK in Europe and the world
- The European Union
- The Commonwealth
- The United Nations

The British Constitution

As a constitutional democracy, the United Kingdom is governed by a wide range of institutions, many of which provide checks on each other's powers. Most of these institutions are of long standing: they include the monarchy, Parliament, (consisting of the House of Commons and the House of Lords), the office of Prime Minister, the Cabinet, the judiciary, the police, the civil service, and the institutions of local government. More recently, devolved administrations have been set up for Scotland, Wales and Northern Ireland. Together, these formal institutions, laws and conventions form the British Constitution. Some people would argue that the roles of other less formal institutions, such as the media and pressure groups, should also be seen as part of the Constitution.

The British Constitution is not written down in any single document, as are the constitutions of many other countries. This is mainly because the United Kingdom has never had a lasting revolution, like America or France, so our most important institutions have been in existence for hundreds of years. Some people believe that there should be a single document, but others believe that an unwritten constitution allows more scope for institutions to adapt to meet changing circumstances and public expectations.

The monarchy

Queen Elizabeth II is the Head of State of the United Kingdom. She is also the monarch or Head of State for many countries in the Commonwealth. The UK, like Denmark, the Netherlands, Norway, Spain and Sweden, has a constitutional monarchy. This means that the king or queen does not rule the country, but appoints the government which the people have chosen in democratic elections. Although the queen or king can advise, warn and encourage the Prime Minister, the decisions on government policies are made by the Prime Minister and Cabinet.

The Queen has reigned since her father's death in 1952. Prince Charles, the Prince of Wales, her oldest son, is the heir to the throne.

The Queen has important ceremonial roles such as the opening of the new parliamentary session each year. On this occasion the Queen makes a speech that summarises the government's policies for the year ahead.

Government

The system of government in the United Kingdom is a parliamentary democracy. The UK is divided into 646 parliamentary constituencies and at least every five years voters in each constituency elect their Member of Parliament (MP) in a general election. All of the elected MPs form the House of Commons. Most MPs belong to a political party and the party with the largest number of MPs forms the government.

The law that requires new elections to Parliament to be held at least every five years is so fundamental that no government has sought to change it. A Bill to change it is the only one to which the House of Lords must give its consent.

Some people argue that the power of Parliament is lessened because of the obligation on the United Kingdom to accept the rules of the European Union and the judgments of the European Court, but it was Parliament itself which created these obligations.

The House of Commons.

The House of Commons is the more important of the two chambers in Parliament, and its members are democratically elected. Nowadays the Prime

Minister and almost all the members of the Cabinet are members of the House of Commons. The members of the House of Commons are called 'Members of Parliament' or MPs for short. Each MP represents a parliamentary constituency, or area of the country: there are 646 of these. MPs have a number of different responsibilities. They represent everyone in their constituency, they help to create new laws, they scrutinise and comment on what the government is doing, and they debate important national issues.

Elections

There must be a general election to elect MPs at least every five years, though they may be held sooner if the Prime Minister so decides. If an MP dies or resigns, there will be another election, called a by-election, in his or her constituency. MPs are elected through a system called 'first past the post'. In each constituency, the candidate who gets the most votes is elected. The government is then formed by the party which wins the majority of constituencies.

The Whips

The Whips are a small group of MPs appointed by their party leaders. They are responsible for discipline in their party and making sure MPs attend the House of Commons to vote. The Chief Whip often attends Cabinet or Shadow Cabinet meetings and arranges the schedule of proceedings in the House of Commons with the Speaker.

European parliamentary elections

Elections for the European Parliament are also held every five years. There are 78 seats for representatives from the UK in the European Parliament and elected members are called Members of the European Parliament (MEPs). Elections to the European Parliament use a system of proportional representation, whereby seats are allocated to each party in proportion to the total votes it won.

The House of Lords

Members of the House of Lords, known as peers, are not elected and do not represent a constituency. The role and membership of the House of Lords have recently undergone big changes. Until 1958 all peers were either 'hereditary', meaning that their titles were inherited, senior judges, or bishops of the Church of England. Since 1958 the Prime Minister has had the power to appoint peers just for their own lifetime. These peers, known as Life Peers, have usually had a distinguished career in politics, business, law or some other profession. This means that debates in the House of Lords often draw on more specialist knowledge than is available to members of the House of Commons. Life Peers are appointed by the Queen on the advice of the Prime Minister, but they include people nominated by the leaders of the other main parties and by an independent Appointments Commission for non-party peers.

In the last few years the hereditary peers have lost the automatic right to attend the House of Lords, although they are allowed to elect a few of their number to represent them.

While the House of Lords is usually the less important of the two chambers of Parliament, it is more independent of the government. It can suggest amendments or propose new laws, which are then discussed by the House of Commons. The House of Lords can become very important if the majority of its members will not agree to pass a law for which the House of Commons has voted. The House of Commons has powers to overrule the House of Lords, but these are very rarely used.

The Prime Minister

The Prime Minister (PM) is the leader of the political party in power. He or she appoints the members of the Cabinet and has control over many important public appointments. The official home of the Prime Minister is 10 Downing Street, in central London, near the Houses of Parliament; he or she also has a country house not far from London called Chequers. The Prime Minister can be changed if the MPs in the governing party decide to do so, or if he or she wishes to resign. More usually, the Prime Minister resigns when his or her party is defeated in a general election.

The Cabinet

The Prime Minister appoints about 20 senior MPs to become ministers in charge of departments. These include the Chancellor of the Exchequer, responsible for the economy, the Home Secretary, responsible for law, order and immigration, the Foreign Secretary, and ministers (called 'Secretaries of State') for education, health and defence. The Lord Chancellor, who is the minister responsible for legal affairs, is also a member of the Cabinet but sat in the House of Lords rather than the House of Commons. Following legislation passed in 2005, it is now possible for the Lord Chancellor to sit in the Commons. These ministers form the Cabinet, a small committee which usually meets weekly and makes important decisions about government policy which often then have to be debated or approved by Parliament.

The Opposition

The second largest party in the House of Commons is called the Opposition. The Leader of the Opposition is the person who hopes to become Prime Minister if his or her party wins the next general election. The Leader of the Opposition leads his or her party in pointing out the government's failures and weaknesses; one important opportunity to do this is at Prime Minister's Questions which takes place every week while Parliament is sitting. The Leader of the Opposition also appoints senior Opposition MPs to lead the criticism of government ministers, and together they form the Shadow Cabinet.

The Speaker

Debates in the House of Commons are chaired by the Speaker, the chief officer of the House of Commons. The Speaker is politically neutral. He or she is an MP, elected by fellow MPs to keep order during political debates and to make sure the rules are followed. This includes making sure the Opposition has a guaranteed amount of time to debate issues it chooses. The Speaker also represents Parliament at ceremonial occasions.

The party system

Under the British system of parliamentary democracy, anyone can stand for election as an MP but they are unlikely to win an election unless they have been nominated to represent one of the major political parties. These are the Labour Party, the Conservative Party, the Liberal Democrats, or one of the parties representing Scottish, Welsh, or Northern Irish interests. There are just a few MPs who do not represent any of the main political parties and are called 'independents'. The main political parties actively seek members among ordinary voters to join their debates, contribute to their costs, and help at elections for Parliament or for local government; they have branches in most constituencies and they hold policy-making conferences every year.

Pressure and lobby groups

Pressure and lobby groups are organisations that try to influence government policy. They play a very important role in politics. There are many pressure groups in the UK. They may represent economic interests (such as the Confederation of British Industry, the Consumers' Association, or the trade unions) or views on particular subjects (e.g. Greenpeace or Liberty). The general public is more likely to support pressure groups than join a political party.

The civil service

Civil servants are managers and administrators who carry out government policy. They have to be politically neutral and professional, regardless of which political party is in power. Although civil servants have to follow the policies of the elected government, they can warn ministers if they think a policy is impractical or not in the public interest. Before a general election takes place, top civil servants study the Opposition party's policies closely in case they need to be ready to serve a new government with different aims and policies.

Devolved administration

In order to give people in Wales and Scotland more control of matters that directly affect them, in 1997 the government began a programme of devolving power from central government. Since 1999 there has been a Welsh Assembly, a Scottish Parliament and, periodically, a Northern Ireland Assembly. Although policy and laws governing defence, foreign affairs, taxation and social security all remain under central UK government control, many other public services now come under the control of the devolved administrations in Wales and Scotland.

Both the Scottish Parliament and Welsh Assembly have been set up using forms of proportional representation which ensures that each party gets a number of seats in proportion to the number of votes they receive. Similarly, proportional representation is used in Northern Ireland in order to ensure 'power sharing' between the Unionist majority (mainly Protestant) and the substantial (mainly Catholic) minority aligned to Irish nationalist parties. A different form of proportional representation is used for elections to the European Parliament.

The Welsh Assembly Government

The National Assembly for Wales, or Welsh Assembly Government (WAG), is situated in Cardiff, the capital city of Wales. It has 60 Assembly Members

(AMs) and elections are held every four years. Members can speak in either Welsh or English and all its publications are in both languages. The Assembly has the power to make decisions on important matters such as education policy, the environment, health services, transport and local government, and to pass laws for Wales on these matters within a statutory framework set out by the UK Parliament at Westminster.

The Parliament of Scotland

A long campaign in Scotland for more independence and democratic control led to the formation in 1999 of the Parliament of Scotland, which sits in Edinburgh, the capital city of Scotland.

There are 129 Members of the Scottish Parliament (MSPs), elected by a form of proportional representation. This has led to the sharing of power in Scotland between the Labour and Liberal Democrat parties. The Scottish Parliament can pass legislation for Scotland on all matters that are not specifically reserved to the UK Parliament. The matters on which the Scottish Parliament can legislate include civil and criminal law, health, education, planning and the raising of additional taxes.

The Northern Ireland Assembly

A Northern Ireland Parliament was established in 1922 when Ireland was divided, but it was abolished in 1972 shortly after the Troubles broke out in 1969.

Soon after the end of the Troubles, the Northern Ireland Assembly was established with a power-sharing agreement which distributes ministerial offices among the main parties. The Assembly has 108 elected members known as MLAs (Members of the Legislative Assembly). Decision-making powers devolved to Northern Ireland include education, agriculture, the environment, health and social services in Northern Ireland.

The UK government kept the power to suspend the Northern Ireland Assembly if the political leaders no longer agreed to work together or if the Assembly was not working in the interests of the people of Northern Ireland. This has happened several times and the Assembly is currently suspended (2006). This means that the elected assembly members do not have power to pass bills or make decisions.

Local government

Towns, cities and rural areas in the UK are governed by democratically elected councils, often called local authorities. Some areas have both district and county councils which have different functions, although most larger towns and cities will have a single local authority. Many councils representing towns and cities appoint a mayor who is the ceremonial leader of the council but in some towns a mayor is appointed to be the effective leader of the administration. London has 33 local authorities, with the Greater London Authority and the Mayor of London co-ordinating policies across the capital. Local authorities are required to provide 'mandatory services' in their area. These services include education, housing, social services, passenger transport, the fire service, rubbish collection, planning, environmental health and libraries.

Most of the money for the local authority services comes from the government through taxes. Only about 20% is funded locally through 'council tax' a local tax set by councils to help pay for local services. It applies to all domestic properties, including houses, bungalows, flats, maisonettes, mobile homes or houseboats, whether owned or rented.

Local elections for councillors are held in May every year. Many candidates stand for council election as members of a political party.

The judiciary

In the UK the laws made by Parliament are the highest authority. But often important questions arise about how the laws are to be interpreted in particular cases. It is the task of the judges (who are together called 'the judiciary') to interpret the law and the government may not interfere with their role. Often the actions of the government are claimed to be illegal and, if the judges agree, then the government must either change its policies or ask Parliament to change the law. This has become all the more important in recent years, as the judges now have the task of applying the Human Rights Act. If they find that a public body is not respecting a person's human rights, they may order that body to change its practices and to pay compensation, if appropriate. If the judges believe that an Act of Parliament is incompatible with the Human Rights Act, they cannot change it themselves but they can ask Parliament to consider doing so.

Judges cannot, however, decide whether people are guilty or innocent of serious crimes. When someone is accused of a serious crime, a jury will decide whether he or she is innocent or guilty and, if guilty, the judge will decide on the penalty. For less important crimes, a magistrate will decide on guilt and on any penalty.

The police

The police service is organised locally, with one police service for each county or group of counties. The largest force is the Metropolitan Police, which serves London and is based at New Scotland Yard. Northern Ireland as a whole is served by the Police Service for Northern Ireland (PSNI). The police have 'operational independence', which means that the government cannot instruct them on what to do in any particular case. But the powers of the police are limited by the law and their finances are controlled by the government and by police authorities made up of councillors and magistrates. The Independent Police Complaints Commission (or, in Northern Ireland, the Police Ombudsman) investigates serious complaints against the police.

Non-departmental public bodies (quangos)

Non-departmental public bodies, also known as quangos, are independent organisations that carry out functions on behalf of the public which it would be inappropriate to place under the political control of a Cabinet minister. There are many hundreds of these bodies, carrying out a wide variety of public duties. Appointments to these bodies are usually made by ministers, but they must do so in an open and fair way.

The role of the media

Proceedings in Parliament are broadcast on digital television and published in official reports such as Hansard, which is available in large libraries and on the internet: www.parliament.uk. Most people, however, get information about political issues and events from newspapers (often called the press), television and radio.

The UK has a free press, meaning that what is written in newspapers is free from government control. Newspaper owners and editors hold strong political opinions and run campaigns to try and influence government policy and public opinion. As a result it is sometimes difficult to distinguish fact from opinion in newspaper coverage.

By law, radio and television coverage of the political parties at election periods must be balanced and so equal time has to be given to rival viewpoints. But broadcasters are free to interview politicians in a tough and lively way.

Who can vote?

The United Kingdom has had a fully democratic system since 1928, when women were allowed to vote at 21, the same age as men. The present voting age of 18 was set in 1969, and (with a few exceptions such as convicted prisoners) all UK-born and naturalised citizens have full civic rights, including the right to vote and do jury service.

Citizens of the UK, the Commonwealth and the Irish Republic (if resident in the UK) can vote in all public elections. Citizens of EU states who are resident in the UK can vote in all elections except national parliamentary (general) elections.

In order to vote in a parliamentary, local or European election, you must have your name on the register of electors, known as the electoral register. If you are eligible to vote, you can register by contacting your local council election registration office. If you don't know what your local authority is, you can find out by telephoning the Local Government Association (LGA) information line on 020 7664 3131 between 9am and 5pm, Monday to Friday. You will have to tell them your postcode or your full address and they will be able to give you the name of your local authority. You can also get voter registration forms in English, Welsh and some other languages on the internet: www.electoralcommission.org.uk.

The electoral register is updated every year in September or October. An electoral registration form is sent to every household and it has to be completed and returned, with the names of everyone who is resident in the household and eligible to vote on 15 October.

In Northern Ireland a different system operates. This is called individual regis-tration and all those entitled to vote must complete their own registration form. Once registered, you can stay on the register provided your personal details do not change. For more information telephone the Electoral Office for Northern Ireland on 028 9044 6688.

By law, each local authority has to make its electoral register available for anyone to look at, although this now has to be supervised. The register is kept at each local electoral registration office (or council office in England and Wales). It is also possible to see the register at some public buildings such as libraries.

Standing for office

Most citizens of the United Kingdom, the Irish Republic or the Commonwealth aged 18 or over can stand for public office. There are some exceptions and these include members of the armed forces, civil servants and people found guilty of certain criminal offences. Members of the House of Lords may not stand for election to the House of Commons but are eligible for all other public offices.

To become a local councillor, a candidate must have a local connection with the area through work, being on the electoral register, or through renting or owning land or property.

Contacting elected members

All elected members have a duty to serve and represent their constituents. You can get contact details for all your representatives and their parties from your local library. Assembly members, MSPs, MPs and MEPs are also listed in the phone book and Yellow Pages. You can contact MPs by letter or phone at their constituency office or their office in the House of Commons: The House of Commons, Westminster, London SW1A OAA, or telephone: 020 7729 3000. Many Assembly Members, MSPs, MPs and MEPs hold regular local 'surgeries'. These are often advertised in the local paper and constituents can go and talk about issues in person. You can find out the name of your local MP and get in touch with them by fax through the website: www.writetothem.com. This service is free.

How to visit Parliament and the Devolved Administrations

The public can listen to debates in the Palace of Westminster from public galleries in both the House of Commons and the House of Lords. You can either write to your local MP in advance to ask for tickets or you can queue on the day at the public entrance. Entrance is free. Sometimes there are long queues for the House of Commons and you may have to wait for at least one or two hours. It is usually easier to get into the House of Lords. You can find further information on the UK Parliament website: www.parliament.uk.

In Northern Ireland, elected members, known as MLAs, meet in the Northern Ireland Assembly at Stormont, in Belfast. The Northern Ireland Assembly is presently suspended. There are two ways to arrange a visit to Stormont. You can either contact the Education Service (details on the Northern Ireland Assembly website: www.niassembly.gov.uk) or contact an MLA

In Scotland, the elected members, called MSPs, meet in the Scottish Parliament at Holyrood in Edinburgh (for more information see: www.scottish.parliament.uk). You can get information, book tickets or arrange tours through the visitor services. You can write to them at The Scottish Parliament, Edinburgh, EH99 1SP, or telephone 0131 348 5200, or email sp.bookings@scottish.parliament.uk.

In Wales, the elected members, known as AMs, meet in the Welsh Assembly in the Senedd in Cardiff Bay (for more information see: www.wales.gov.uk). You can book guided tours or seats in the public galleries for the Welsh Assembly. To make a booking, telephone the Assembly booking line on 029 2089 8477 or email: assembly.booking@wales.gsi.gov.uk.

Check that you understand:

- The role of the monarchy
- How Parliament works, and the difference between the House of Commons and the House of Lords
- How often general elections are held
- Where the official residence of the Prime Minister is
- The role of the Cabinet and who is in it
- The nature of the UK Constitution
- The job of the Opposition, the Leader of the Opposition and the Shadow Cabinet
- The difference between 'first past the post' and proportional repre-sentation
- The form of electoral systems in the devolved administrations in Northern Ireland, Scotland and Wales
- The rights and duties of British citizens, including naturalised citizens
- How the judiciary, police and local authorities work
- What non-departmental public bodies are

31

The UK in Europe and the world

The Commonwealth

The Commonwealth is an association of countries, most of which were once part of the British Empire, though a few countries that were not in the Empire have also joined it.

Commonwealth members

Antigua and Barbuda
Australia
The Bahamas
Bangladesh
Barbados
Belize
Botswana
Brunei Darussalam
Cameroon
Canada
Cyprus
Dominica
Fiji Islands
The Gambia
Ghana
Grenada
Guyana
India
Jamaica
Kenya
Kiribati
Lesotho
Malawi
Malaysia
Maldives
Malta
Mauritius
Mozambique

Namibia
Nauru*
New Zealand
Nigeria
Pakistan
Papua New Guinea
St Kitts and Nevis
St Lucia
St Vincent and the Grenadines
Samoa
Seychelles
Sierra Leone
Singapore
Solomon Islands
South Africa
Sri Lanka
Swaziland
Tonga
Trinidad and Tobago
Tuvalu
Uganda
United Kingdom
United Republic of Tanzania
Vanuatu
Zambia

*Nauru is a Special Member.

The Queen is the head of the Commonwealth, which currently has 53 member states. Membership is voluntary and the Commonwealth has no power over its members although it can suspend membership. The Commonwealth aims to promote democracy, good government and to eradicate poverty.

The European Union (EU)

The European Union (EU), originally called the European Economic Community (EEC), was set up by six Western European countries who signed the Treaty of Rome on 25 March 1957. One of the main reasons for doing this was the belief that co-operation between states would reduce the likelihood of another war in Europe. Originally the UK decided not to join this group and only became part of the European Union in 1973. In 2004 ten new member countries joined the EU, with a further two in 2006 making a total of 27 member countries.

One of the main aims of the EU today is for member states to function as a single market. Most of the countries of the EU have a shared currency, the euro, but the UK has decided to retain its own currency unless the British people choose to accept the euro in a referendum. Citizens of an EU member state have the right to travel to and work in any EU country if they have a valid passport or identity card. This right can be restricted on the grounds of public health, public order and public security. The right to work is also sometimes restricted for citizens of countries that have joined the EU recently.

The Council of the European Union (usually called the Council of Ministers) is effectively the governing body of the EU. It is made up of government ministers from each country in the EU and, together with the European Parliament, is the legislative body of the EU. The Council of Ministers passes EU law on the recommendations of the European Commission and the European Parliament and takes the most important decisions about how the EU is run. The European Commission is based in Brussels, the capital city of Belgium. It is the civil service of the EU and drafts proposals for new EU policies and laws and administers its funding programmes.

The European Parliament meets in Strasbourg, in north-eastern France, and in Brussels. Each country elects members, called Members of the European Parliament (MEPs), every five years. The European Parliament examines decisions made by the European Council and the European Commission, and it has the power to refuse agreement to European laws proposed by the Commission and to check on the spending of EU funds.

European Union law is legally binding in the UK and all the other member states. European laws, called directives, regulations or framework decisions, have made a lot of difference to people's rights in the UK, particularly at work. For example, there are EU directives about the procedures for making workers redundant, and regulations that limit the number of hours people can be made to work.

The Council of Europe

The Council of Europe was created in 1949 and the UK was one of the founder members. Most of the countries of Europe are members. It has no power to make laws but draws up conventions and charters which focus on human rights, democracy, education, the environment, health and culture. The most important of these is the European Convention on Human Rights; all member states are bound by this Convention and a member state which persistently refuses to obey the Convention may be expelled from the Council of Europe.

The United Nations (UN)

The UK is a member of the United Nations (UN), an international organisation to which over 190 countries now belong. The UN was set up after the Second World War and aims to prevent war and promote international peace and security. There are 15 members on the UN Security Council, which recommends action by the UN when there are international crises and threats to peace. The UK is one of the five permanent members.

Three very important agreements produced by the UN are the Universal Declaration of Human Rights, the Convention on the Elimination of All Forms of Discrimination against Women, and the UN Convention on the Rights of the Child. Although none of these has the force of law, they are widely used in political debate and legal cases to reinforce the law and to assess the behaviour of countries.

Check that you understand:

- The differences between the Council of Europe, the European Union, the European Commission and the European Parliament
- The UK is a member of the Council of Europe and the European Union
- The EU aims to become a single market and it is administered by a Council of Ministers of governments of member states
- Subject to some restrictions, EU citizens may travel to and work in any EU country
- The roles of the UN and the commonwealth

EVERYDAY NEEDS

In this chapter there is information about:

- Housing
- Services in and for the home
- Money and credit
- Health
- Pregnancy and care of young children
- Education
- Leisure
- Travel and transport
- Identity documents

Housing

Buying a home

Two-thirds of people in the UK own their own home. Most other people rent houses, flats or rooms.

Mortgages

People who buy their own home usually pay for it with a mortgage, a special loan from a bank or building society. This loan is paid back, with interest, over a long period of time, usually 25 years. You can get information about mortgages from a bank or building society. Some banks can also give information about Islamic (Sharia) mortgages.

If you are having problems paying your mortgage repayments, you can get help and advice. It is important to speak to your bank or building society as soon as you can.

Estate agents

If you wish to buy a home, usually the first place to start is an estate agent. In Scotland the process is different and you should go first to a solicitor. Estate agents represent the person selling their house or flat. They arrange for buyers to visit homes that are for sale. There are estate agents in all towns and cities and they usually have websites where they advertise the homes for sale. You can also find details about homes for sale on the internet and in national and local newspapers.

Making an offer

In the UK, except in Scotland, when you find a home you wish to buy you have to make an offer to the seller. You usually do this through an estate agent or solicitor. Many people offer a lower price than the seller is asking. Your first offer must be 'subject to contract' so that you can withdraw if there are reasons why you cannot complete the purchase. In Scotland the seller sets a price and buyers make offers over that amount. The agreement becomes legally binding earlier than it does elsewhere in the UK.

Solicitor and surveyor

It is important that a solicitor helps you through the process of buying a house or flat. When you make an offer on a property, the solicitor will carry out a number of legal checks on the property, the seller and the local area. The solicitor will provide the legal agreements necessary for you to buy the property. The bank or building society that is providing you with your mortgage will also carry out checks on the house or flat you wish to buy. These are done by a surveyor. The buyer does not usually see the result of this survey, so the buyer often asks a second surveyor to check the house as well. In Scotland the survey is carried out before an offer is made, to help people decide how much they want to bid for the property.

Rented accommodation

It is possible to rent accommodation from the local authority (the council), from a housing association or from private property owners called landlords.

The local authority

Most local authorities (or councils) provide housing. This is often called 'council housing'. In Northern Ireland social housing is provided by the Northern Ireland Housing Executive (www.nihe.co.uk). In Scotland you can find information on social housing at: www.sfha.co.uk. Everyone is entitled to apply for council accommodation. To apply you must put your name on the council register or list. This is available from the housing department at the local authority. You are then assessed according to your needs. This is done through a system of

36

points. You get more points if you have priority needs, for example if you are homeless and have children or chronic ill health.

It is important to note that in many areas of the UK there is a shortage of council accommodation, and that some people have to wait a very long time for a house or flat.

Housing associations

Housing associations are independent not-for-profit organisations which provide housing for rent. In some areas they have taken over the administration of local authority housing. They also run schemes called shared ownership, which help people buy part of a house or flat if they cannot afford to buy all of it at once. There are usually waiting lists for homes owned by housing associations.

Privately rented accommodation

Many people rent houses or flats privately, from landlords. Information about private accommodation can be found in local newspapers, notice boards, estate agents and letting agents.

Tenancy agreement

When you rent a house or flat privately you sign a tenancy agreement, or lease. This explains the conditions or 'rules' you must follow while renting the property. This agreement must be checked very carefully to avoid problems later. The agreement also contains a list of any furniture or fittings in the property. This is called an inventory. Before you sign the agreement, check the details and keep it safe during your tenancy.

Deposit and rent

You will probably be asked to give the landlord a deposit at the beginning of your tenancy. This is to cover the cost of any damage. It is usually equal to one month's rent. The landlord must return this money to you at the end of your tenancy, unless you have caused damage to the property.

Your rent is fixed with your landlord at the beginning of the tenancy. The landlord cannot raise the rent without your agreement.

If you have a low income or are unemployed you may be able to claim Housing Benefit (see Help) to help you pay your rent.

Renewing and ending a tenancy

Your tenancy agreement will be for a fixed period of time, often six months. After this time the tenancy can be ended or, if both tenant and landlord agree, renewed. If you end the tenancy before the fixed time, you usually have to pay the rent for the agreed full period of the tenancy.

A landlord cannot force a tenant to leave. If a landlord wishes a tenant to leave they must follow the correct procedures. These vary according to the type of tenancy. It is a criminal offence for a landlord to use threats or violence against a tenant or to force them to leave without an order from court.

Discrimination

It is unlawful for a landlord to discriminate against someone looking for accommodation because of their sex, race, nationality, or ethnic group, or because they are disabled, unless the landlord or a close relative of the landlord is sharing the accommodation.

Homelessness

If you are homeless you should go for help to the local authority (or, in Northern Ireland, the Housing Executive). They have a legal duty to offer help and advice, but will not offer you a place to live unless you have priority need (see above) and have a connection with the area, such as work or family. You must also show that you have not made yourself intentionally homeless.

Help

If you are homeless or have problems with your landlord, help can be found from the following:

- The housing department of the local authority will give advice on homelessness and on Housing Benefit as well as deal with problems you may have in council-owned property

- The Citizens Advice Bureau will give advice on all types of housing problems. There may also be a housing advice centre in your neighbourhood

- Shelter is a housing charity which runs a 24-hour helpline on 0808 800 4444, or visit www.shelternet.org.uk

- Help with the cost of moving and setting up home may be available from the Social Fund. This is run by the Department for Work and Pensions (DWP). It provides grants and loans such as the Community Care Grant for people setting up home after being homeless or after they have been in prison or other institutions. Other loans are available for people who have had an emergency such as flooding. Information about these is available at the Citizens Advice Bureau or Jobcentre Plus.

Services in and for the home

Water

Water is supplied to all homes in the UK. The charge for this is called the water rates. When you move in to a new home (bought or rented), you should receive a letter telling you the name of the company responsible for supplying your water. The water rates may be paid in one payment (a lump sum) or in instalments, usually monthly. If you receive Housing Benefit, you should check to see if this covers the water rates. The cost of the water usually depends on the size of your property, but some homes have a water meter which tells you exactly how much water you have used. In Northern Ireland water is currently (2006) included in the domestic rates (see Council tax), although this may change in future.

Electricity and gas

All properties in the UK have electricity supplied at 240 volts. Most homes also have gas. When you move into a new home or leave an old one, you should make a note of the electricity and gas meter readings. If you have an urgent problem with your gas, electricity or water supply, you can ring a 24-hour helpline. This can be found on your bill, in the Yellow Pages or in the phone book.

Gas and electricity suppliers

It is possible to choose between different gas and electricity suppliers. These have different prices and different terms and conditions. Get advice before you sign a contract with a new supplier. To find out which company supplies your gas, telephone Transco on 0870 608 1524

To find out which company supplies your electricity, telephone Energywatch on 0845 906 0708 or visit www.energywatch.org.uk. Energywatch can also give you advice on changing your supplier of electricity or gas.

Telephone

Most homes already have a telephone line (called a land line). If you need a new line, telephone BT on 150 442, or contact a cable company. Many companies offer land line, mobile telephone and broadband internet services. You can get advice about prices or about changing your company from Ofcom at: www.ofcom.org.uk. You can call from public payphones using cash, pre-paid phone cards or credit or debit cards. Calls made from hotels and hostels are usually more expensive. Dial 999 or 112 for emergency calls for police, fire or ambulance service. These calls are free. Do not use these numbers if it is not a real emergency; you can always find the local numbers for these services in the phone book.

Bills

Information on how to pay for water, gas, electricity and the telephone is found on the back of each bill. If you have a bank account you can pay your bills by standing order or direct debit. Most companies operate a budget scheme which allows you to pay a fixed sum every month. If you do not pay a bill, the service can be cut off. To get a service reconnected, you have to pay another charge.

Refuse collection

Refuse is also called waste, or rubbish. The local authority collects the waste regularly, usually on the same day of each week. Waste must be put outside in a particular place to get collected. In some parts of the country the waste is put into plastic bags, in others it is put into bins with wheels. In many places you must recycle your rubbish, separating paper, glass, metal or plastic from the other rubbish. Large objects which you want to throw away, such as a bed, a wardrobe or a fridge, need to be collected separately. Contact the local authority to arrange this. If you have a business, such as a factory or a shop, you must make special arrangements with the local authority for your waste to be collected. It is a criminal offence to dump rubbish anywhere.

Council Tax

Local government services, such as education, police, roads, refuse collection and libraries, are paid for partly by grants from the government and partly by

Council Tax. In Northern Ireland there is a system of domestic rates instead of the Council Tax. The amount of Council Tax you pay depends on the size and value of your house or flat (dwelling). You must register to pay Council Tax when you move into a new property, either as the owner or the tenant. You can pay the tax in one payment, in two instalments, or in ten instalments (from April to January).

If only one person lives in the flat or house, you get a 25% reduction on your Council Tax. (This does not apply in Northern Ireland). You may also get a reduction if someone in the property has a disability. People on a low income or who receive benefits such as Income Support or Jobseeker's Allowance can get Council Tax Benefit. You can get advice on this from the local authority or the Citizens Advice Bureau.

Buildings and household insurance

If you buy a home with a mortgage, you must insure the building against fire, theft and accidental damage. The landlord should arrange insurance for rented buildings. It is also wise to insure your possessions against theft or damage. There are many companies that provide insurance.

Neighbours

If you live in rented accommodation, you will have a tenancy agreement. This explains all the conditions of your tenancy. It will probably include information on what to do if you have problems with your housing. Occasionally, there may be problems with your neighbours. If you do have problems with your neighbours, they can usually be solved by speaking to them first. If you cannot solve the problem, speak to your landlord, local authority or housing association. Keep a record of the problems in case you have to show exactly what the problems are and when they started. Neighbours who cause a very serious nuisance may be taken to court and can be evicted from their home.

There are several mediation organisations which help neighbours to solve their disputes without having to go to court. Mediators talk to both sides and try to find a solution acceptable to both. You can get details of mediation organisations from the local authority, Citizens Advice, and Mediation UK on 0117 904 6661 or visit: www.mediationuk.co.uk.

Money and credit

Bank notes in the UK come in denominations (values) of £5, £10, £20 and £50. Northern Ireland and Scotland have their own bank notes which are valid everywhere in the UK, though sometimes people may not realise this and may not wish to accept them.

The euro

In January 2002 twelve European Union (EU) states adopted the euro as their common currency. The UK government decided not to adopt the euro at that time, and has said it will only do so if the British people vote for the euro in a referendum. The euro does circulate to some extent in Northern Ireland, particularly in the towns near the border with Ireland.

Foreign currency

You can get or change foreign currency at banks, building societies, large post offices and exchange shops or bureaux de change. You might have to order some currencies in advance. The exchange rates vary and you should check for the best deal.

Banks and building societies

Most adults in the UK have a bank or building society account. Many large national banks or building societies have branches in towns and cities throughout the UK. It is worth checking the different types of account each

42

one offers. Many employers pay salaries directly into a bank or building society account. There are many banks and building societies to choose from. To open an account, you need to show documents to prove your identity, such as a passport, immigration document or driving licence. You also need to show something with your address on it like a tenancy agreement or household bill. It is also possible to open bank accounts in some supermarkets or on the internet.

Cash and debit cards

Cash cards allow you to use cash machines to withdraw money from your account. For this you need a Personal Identification Number (PIN) which you must keep secret. A debit card allows you to pay for things without using cash. You must have enough money in your account to cover what you buy. If you lose your cash card or debit card you must inform the bank immediately.

Credit and store cards

Credit cards can be used to buy things in shops, on the telephone and over the internet. A store card is like a credit card but used only in a specific shop. Credit and store cards do not draw money from your bank account, but you will be sent a bill every month. If you do not pay the total amount on the bill, you are charged interest. Although credit and store cards are useful, the interest is usually very high and many people fall into debt this way. If you lose your credit or store cards you must inform the company immediately.

Credit and loans

People in the UK often borrow money from banks and other organisations to pay for things like household goods, cars and holidays. This is more common in the UK than in many other countries. You must be very sure of the terms and conditions when you decide to take out a loan. You can get advice on loans from the Citizens Advice Bureau if you are uncertain.

Being refused credit

Banks and other organisations use different information about you to make a decision about a loan, such as your occupation, address, salary and previous credit record. If you apply for a loan you might be refused. If this happens, you have the right to ask the reason why.

Credit unions

Credit unions are financial co-operatives owned and controlled by their members. The members pool their savings and then make loans from this pool. Interest rates in credit unions are usually lower than banks and building societies. There are credit unions in many cities and towns. To find the nearest credit union contact the Association of British Credit Unions (ABCUL) on: www.abcul.coop.

Insurance

As well as insuring their property and possessions (see above), many people insure their credit cards and mobile phones. They also buy insurance when they travel abroad in case they lose their luggage or need medical treatment. Insurance is compulsory if you have a car or motorcycle. You can usually arrange insurance directly with an insurance company, or you can use a broker who will help you get the best deal.

Social security

The UK has a system of social security which pays welfare benefits to people who do not have enough money to live on. Benefits are usually available for the sick and disabled, older people, the unemployed and those on low incomes. People who do not have legal rights of residence (or 'settlement') in the UK cannot usually receive benefits. Arrangements for paying and receiving benefits are complex because they have to cover people in many different situations. Guides to benefits are available from Jobcentre Plus offices, local libraries, post offices and the Citizens Advice Bureau.

Check that you understand:

- What you need to open a bank or building society account
- What debit, credit and store cards are
- What a credit union is
- What insurance is
- How to get help with benefits and problems with debt

Health

Healthcare in the UK is organised under the National Health Service (NHS). The NHS began in 1948, and is one of the largest organisations in Europe. It provides all residents with free healthcare and treatment.

Finding a doctor

Family doctors are called General Practitioners (GPs) and they work in surgeries. GPs often work together in a group practice. This is sometimes called a Primary Health Care Centre.

Your GP is responsible for organising the health treatment you receive. Treatment can be for physical and mental illnesses. If you need to see a specialist, you must go to your GP first. Your GP will then refer you to a specialist in a hospital. Your GP can also refer you for specialist treatment if you have special needs.

You can get a list of local GPs from libraries, post offices, the tourist information office, the Citizens Advice Bureau, the local Health Authority and from the following websites:

www.nhs.uk/ for health practitioners in England;
www.wales.nhs.uk/directory.cfm for health practitioners in Wales;
www.n-i.nhs.uk for health practitioners in Northern Ireland;
www.show.scot.nhs.uk/findnearest/healthservices in Scotland.
You can also ask neighbours and friends for the name of their local doctor.

You can attend a hospital without a GP's letter only in the case of an emergency. If you have an emergency you should go to the Accident and Emergency (A & E) department of the nearest hospital.

Registering with a GP

You should look for a GP as soon as you move to a new area. You should not wait until you are ill. The health centre, or surgery, will tell you what you need to do to register. Usually you must have a medical card. If you do not have one, the GP's receptionist should give you a form to send to the local health authority. They will then send you a medical card.

Before you register you should check the surgery can offer what you need. For example, you might need a woman GP, or maternity services. Sometimes GPs have many patients and are unable to accept new ones. If you cannot find a GP, you can ask your local health authority to help you find one.

Using your doctor

All patients registering with a GP are entitled to a free health check. Appointments to see the GP can be made by phone or in person. Sometimes you might have to wait several days before you can see a doctor. If you need immediate medical attention ask for an urgent appointment. You should go to the GP's surgery a few minutes before the appointment. If you cannot attend or do not need the appointment any more, you must let the surgery know. The GP needs patients to answer all questions as fully as possible in order to find out what is wrong. Everything you tell the GP is completely confidential and cannot be passed on to anyone else without your permission. If you do not understand something, ask for clarification. If you have difficulties with English, bring someone who can help you, or ask the receptionist for an interpreter. This must be done when you make the appointment. If you have asked for an interpreter, it is important that you keep your appointment because this service is expensive.

In exceptional circumstances, GPs can visit patients at home but they always give priority to people who are unable to travel. If you call the GP outside normal working hours, you will have to answer several questions about your situation. This is to assess how serious your case is. You will then be told if a doctor can come to your home. You might be advised to go to the nearest A & E department.

Charges

Treatment from the GP is free but you have to pay a charge for your medicines and for certain services, such as vaccinations for travel abroad. If the GP decides you need to take medicine you will be given a prescription. You must take this to a pharmacy (chemist).

Prescriptions

Prescriptions are free for anyone who is

- under 16 years of age (under 25 in Wales)
- under 19 and in full-time education
- aged 60 or over
- pregnant or with baby under 12 months old

- suffering from a specified medical condition
- receiving Income Support, jobseekers' Allowance, Working Families or Disabilities Tax Credit

Feeling unwell

If you or your child feels unwell you have the following options:

For information or advice

- ask your local pharmacist (chemist). The pharmacy can give advice on medicines and some illnesses and conditions that are not serious
- speak to a nurse by phoning NHS Direct on 0845 46 47
- use the NHS Direct website, NHS Direct Online: www.nhsdirect.nhs.uk

To see a doctor or nurse

- make an appointment to see your GP or a nurse working in the surgery
- visit an NHS walk-in centre

For urgent medical treatment

- contact your GP
- go to your nearest hospital with an Accident and Emergency department
- call 999 for an ambulance. Calls are free. ONLY use this service for a real emergency.

NHS Direct is a 24-hour telephone service which provides information on particular health conditions. Telephone: 0845 46 47. You may ask for an interpreter for advice in your own language. In Scotland, NHS24 at: www.nhs24.com telephone 08454 24 24 24.

NHS Direct Online is a website providing information about health services and several medical conditions and treatments: www.nhsdirect.nhs.uk.

NHS walk-in centres provide treatment for minor injuries and illnesses seven days a week. You do not need an appointment. For details of your nearest centre call NHS Direct or visit the NHS website at: www.nhs.uk (for Northern Ireland www.n-i.nhs.uk) and click on 'local NHS services'.

Going into hospital

If you need minor tests at a hospital, you will probably attend the Outpatients department. If your treatment takes several hours, you will go into hospital as a day patient. If you need to stay overnight, you will go into hospital as an in-patient.

You should take personal belongings with you, such as a towel, night clothes, things for washing, and a dressing gown. You will receive all your meals while you are an in-patient. If you need advice about going into hospital, contact Customer Services or the Patient Advice and Liaison Service (PALS) at the hospital where you will receive treatment.

Dentists

You can get the name of a dentist by asking at the local library, at the Citizens Advice Bureau and through NHS Direct. Most people have to pay for dental treatment. Some dentists work for the NHS and some are private. NHS dentists charge less than private dentists, but some dentists have two sets of charges, both NHS and private. A dentist should explain your treatment and the charges before the treatment begins.

Free dental treatment is available to

- people under 18 (in Wales people under 25 and over 60)
- pregnant women and women with babies under 12 months old
- people on income support, Jobseekers' Allowance or Pension Credit Guarantee

Opticians

Most people have to pay for sight tests and glasses, except children, people over 60, people with certain eye conditions and people receiving certain benefits. In Scotland, eye tests are free.

Pregnancy and care of young children

If you are pregnant you will receive regular ante-natal care. This is available from your local hospital, local health centre or from special antenatal clinics.

You will receive support from a GP and from a midwife. Midwives work in hospitals or health centres. Some GPs do not provide maternity services so you may wish to look for another GP during your pregnancy. In the UK women usually have their babies in hospital, especially if it is their first baby. It is common for the father to attend the birth, but only if the mother wants him to be there.

A short time after you have your child, you will begin regular contact with a health visitor. She or he is a qualified nurse and can advise you about caring for your baby. The first visits will be in your home, but after that you might meet the health visitor at a clinic. You can ask advice from your health visitor until your child is five years old. In most towns and cities there are mother and toddler groups or playgroups for small children. These often take place at local churches and community centres. You might be able to send your child to a nursery school (see Going to school).

Information on pregnancy

You can get information on maternity and ante-natal services in your area from your local health authority, a health visitor or your GP. The number of your health authority will be in the phone book.

The Family Planning Association (FPA) gives advice on contraception and sexual health. The FPA's helpline is 0845 310 1334, or: www.fpa.org.uk.

The National Childbirth Trust gives information and support in pregnancy, childbirth and early parenthood: www.nctpregnancyandbabycare.com.

Registering a birth

Your must register your baby with the Registrar of Births, Marriages and Deaths (Register Office) within six weeks of the birth. The address of your local Register Office is in the phone book. If the parents are married, either the mother or father can register the birth. If they are not married, only the mother can register the birth. If the parents are not married but want both names on the child's birth certificate, both mother and father must be present when they register their baby.

Education

Going to school

Education in the UK is free and compulsory for all children between the ages of 5 and 16 (4 to 16 in Northern Ireland). The education system varies in England, Scotland, Wales and Northern Ireland.

The child's parent or guardian is responsible for making sure their child goes to school, arrives on time and attends for the whole school year. If they do not do this, the parent or guardian may be prosecuted.

Some areas of the country offer free nursery education for children over the age of 3. In most parts of the UK, compulsory education is divided into two stages, primary and secondary. In some places there is a middle-school system. In England and Wales the primary stage lasts from 5 to 11, in Scotland from 5 to 12 and in Northern Ireland from 4 to 11. The secondary stage lasts until the age of 16. At that age young people can choose to leave school or to continue with their education until they are 17 or 18.

Details of local schools are available from your local education authority office or website. The addresses and phone numbers of local education authorities are in the phone book.

Primary schools

These are usually schools where both boys and girls learn together and are usually close to a child's home. Children tend to be with the same group and teacher all day. Schools encourage parents to help their children with learning, particularly with reading and writing.

Secondary schools

At age 11 (12 in Scotland) children go to secondary school. This might normally be the school nearest their home, but parents in England and Wales are allowed to express a preference for a different school. In some areas, getting a secondary school place in a preferred school can be difficult, and parents often apply to several schools in order to make sure their child gets offered a place. In Northern Ireland many schools select children through a test taken at the age of 11.

If the preferred school has enough places, the child will be offered a place. If there are not enough places, children will be offered places according to the school's admission arrangements. Admission arrangements vary from area to area.

Secondary schools are larger than primary schools. Most are mixed sex, although there are single sex schools in some areas. Your local education authority will give you information on schools in your area. It will also tell you which schools have spaces and give you information about why some children will be given places when only a few are available and why other children might not. It will also tell you how to apply for a secondary school place.

Costs

Education at state schools in the UK is free, but parents have to pay for school uniforms and sports wear. There are sometimes extra charges for music lessons and for school outings. Parents on low incomes can get help with costs, and with the cost of school meals. You can get advice on this from the local education authority or the Citizens Advice Bureau.

Church and other faith schools

Some primary and secondary schools in the UK are linked to the Church of England or the Roman Catholic Church. These are called 'faith schools'. In some areas there are Muslim, Jewish and Sikh schools. In Northern Ireland, some schools are called Integrated Schools. These schools aim to bring children of different religions together. Information on faith schools is available from your local education authority.

Independent schools

Independent schools are private schools. They are not run or paid for by the state. Independent secondary schools are also sometimes called public schools. There are about 2,500 independent schools in the UK. About 8% of children go to these schools. At independent schools parents must pay the full cost of their child's education. Some independent schools offer scholarships which pay some or all of the costs of the child's education.

The school curriculum

All state, primary and secondary schools in England, Wales and Northern Ireland follow the National Curriculum. This covers English, maths, science, design and technology, information and communication technology (ICT), history, geography, modern foreign languages, art and design, music, physical education (PE) and citizenship. In Wales, children learn Welsh.

In some primary schools in Wales, all the lessons are taught in Welsh. In Scotland, pupils follow a broad curriculum informed by national guidance. Schools must, by law, provide religious education (RE) to all pupils. Parents are allowed to withdraw their children from these lessons. RE lessons have a Christian basis but children also learn about the other major religions.

Assessment

In England, the curriculum is divided into four stages, called Key Stages. After each stage children are tested. They take Key Stage tests (also called SATs) at ages 7, 11 and 14. At 16 they usually take the General Certificates of Secondary Education (GCSEs) in several subjects, although some schools also offer other qualifications. At 18, young people who have stayed at school do AGCEs (Advanced GCE levels) often just called A levels.

In Wales, schools follow the Welsh National Curriculum but have abolished national tests for children at age 7 and 11. There are also plans in Wales to stop testing children at 14. Teachers in Wales still have to assess and report on their pupils' progress and achievements at 7 and 11.

In Scotland, the curriculum is divided into two phases. The first phase is from 5 to 14. There are six levels in this phase, levels A to F. There are no tests for whole groups during this time. Teachers test individual children when they are ready. From 14 to 16, young people do Standard Grade. After 16 they can study at Intermediate, Higher or Advanced level. In Scotland there will soon be a single curriculum for all pupils from age 3 to age 18. This is called A Curriculum for Excellence. More information can be found at: www.acurriculumforexcellencescotland.gov.uk.

Help with English

If your child's main language is not English, the school may arrange for extra language support from an EAL (English Additional Language) specialist teacher.

Careers education

All children get careers advice from the age of 14. Advice is also available from Connexions, a national service for young people: telephone 080 800 13219 or: www.connexions-direct.com in England. In Wales, Careers Wales offers advice to children from the age of 11. For further information visit: www.careerswales.com or telephone 0800 100 900.

In Scotland, Careers Scotland provides information, services and support to all ages and stages. For further information visit: www.careers-scotland.org.uk or telephone 0845 8 502 502.

Parents and schools

Many parents are involved with their child's school. A number of places on a school's governing body are reserved for parents. The governing body decides how the school is run and administered and produces reports on the progress of the school from year to year. In Scotland, parents can be members of school boards or parent councils.

Schools must be open 190 days a year. Term dates are decided by the governing body or by the local education authority. Children must attend the whole school year. Schools expect parents and guardians to inform them if their child is going to be absent from school. All schools ask parents to sign a home-school agreement. This is a list of things that both the school and the parent or guardian agrees to do to ensure a good education for the child. All parents receive a report every year on their child's progress. They also have the chance to go to the school to talk to their child's teachers.

Further education and adult education

At 16, young people can leave school or stay on to do A levels (Higher grades in Scotland) in preparation for university. Some young people go to their local further education (FE) college to improve their exam grades or to get new qualifications for a career. Most courses are free up to the age of 19. Young people from families with low incomes can get financial help with their studies when they leave school at 16. This is called the Education Maintenance Allowance (EMA). Information about this is available at your local college or at: www.dfes.gov.uk.

Further education colleges also offer courses to adults over the age of 18. These include courses for people wishing to improve their skills in English. These courses are called ESOL (English for Speakers of Other Languages). There are also courses for English speakers who need to improve their literacy and numeracy and for people who need to learn new skills for employment. ESOL courses are also available in community centres and training centres. There is sometimes a waiting list for ESOL courses because demand is high. In England and Wales, ESOL, literacy and numeracy courses are also called Skills for Life courses. You can get information at your local college or local library or from learndirect on 0800 100 900.

Many people join other adult education classes to learn a new skill or hobby and to meet new people. Classes are very varied and range from sports to learning a musical instrument or a new language. Details are usually available from your local library, college or adult education centre.

University

More young people go to university now than in the past. Many go after A levels (or Higher grades in Scotland) at age 18 but it is also possible to go to university later in life. At present, most students in England, Wales and Northern Ireland have to pay towards the cost of their tuition fees and to pay for their living expenses. In Scotland there are no tuition fees but after students finish university they pay back some of the cost of their education in a payment called an endowment. At present, universities can charge up to £3,000 per year for their tuition fees, but students do not have to pay anything towards their fees before or during their studies, The government pays their tuition fees and then charges for them when a student starts working after university. Some families on low incomes receive help with their children's tuition fees.

This is called a grant. The universities also give help, in the form of bursaries. Most students get a low-interest student loan from a bank. This pays for their living costs while they are at university. When a student finishes university and starts working, he or she must pay back the loan.

> **Check that you understand:**
>
> - The different stages of a child's education
> - That there are differences in the education systems in England, Scotland, Wales and Northern Ireland
> - That there are different kinds of school, and that some of them charge fees
> - What the national curriculum is
> - What the governing body of a school does
> - Options for young people at the age of 16
> - Courses available at FE colleges
> - Where you can get English classes or other education for adults, including university

Leisure

Information

Information about theatre, cinema, music and exhibitions is found in local newspapers, local libraries and tourist information offices. Many museums and art galleries are free.

Film, video and DVD

Films in the UK have a system to show if they are suitable for children. This is called the classification system, if a child is below the age of the classification, they should not watch the film at a cinema or on DVD. All films receive a classification, as follows:

U (Universal):   suitable for anyone aged 4 years and over

PG (parental guidance): suitable for everyone but some parts of the film might be unsuitable for children. Their parents should decide.

12 or 12a: children under 12 are not allowed to see or rent the film unless they are with an adult.

15:	children under 15 are not allowed to see or rent the film.
18:	no one under 18 is allowed to see or rent the film.
R18:	no one under 18 is allowed to see the film, which is only available in specially licensed cinemas.

Television and radio

Anyone in the UK with a television (TV), DVD or video recorder, computer or any device which is used for watching or recording TV programmes must be covered by a valid television licence. One licence covers all of the equipment at one address, but people who rent different rooms in a shared house must each buy a separate licence.

A colour TV licence currently costs £131.50 (2006) and lasts for 12 months. People aged 75, or over can apply for a free TV licence. Blind people can claim a 50% discount on their TV licence. You risk prosecution and a fine if you watch TV but are not covered by a TV licence. There are many ways to buy a TV licence including from local Pay Point outlets or on-line at: www.tvlicensing.co.uk. It is also possible to pay for the licence in instalments. For more information telephone 0870 576 3763 or write to TV Licensing, Bristol BS981TL

Sports, clubs and societies

Information about local clubs and societies can usually be found at local libraries or through your local authority. For information about sports you should ask in the local leisure centre. Libraries and leisure centres often organise activities for children during the school holidays.

Places of interest

The UK has a large network of public footpaths in the countryside. Many parts of the countryside and places of interest are kept open by the National Trust. This is a charity that works to preserve important buildings and countryside in the UK. Information about National Trust buildings and areas open to the public is available on: www.nationaltrust.org.uk.

Pubs and night clubs

Public houses, or pubs, are an important part of social life in the UK. To drink alcohol in a pub you must be 18 or over. People under 18 are not allowed to buy alcohol in a supermarket or in an off-licence either. The landlord of the pub may allow people of 14 to come into the pub but they are not allowed to drink. At 16, people can drink wine or beer with a meal in a hotel or restaurant.

Pubs are usually open during the day and until 11 pm. If a pub wants to stay open later, it must apply for a special licence. Night clubs open and close later than pubs.

Betting and gambling

People under 18 are not allowed into betting shops or gambling clubs. There is a National Lottery for which draws, with large prizes, are made every week. You can enter by buying a ticket or a scratch card. People under 16 are not allowed to buy a lottery ticket or scratch card.

Pets

Many people in the UK have pets such as cats and dogs. It is against the law to treat a pet cruelly or to neglect it. All dogs in public places must wear a collar showing the name and address of the owner. The owner is responsible for keeping the dog under control and for cleaning up after the animal in a public place. Vaccinations and medical treatment for animals are available from veterinary surgeons (vets). If you cannot afford to pay a vet, you can go to a charity called the PDSA (People's Dispensary for Sick Animals). To find your nearest branch, visit: www.pdsa.org.uk.

Travel and transport

Trains, buses and coaches

For information about trains telephone the National Rail Enquiry Service: 08457 48 49 50, or visit: www.nationalrail.co.uk. For trains in Northern Ireland, phone Translink on 028 90 66 66 30 or visit: www.translink.co.uk. For information about local bus times phone 0870 608 250. For information on coaches, tele- phone National Express on 08705 80 80 80, or visit: www.nationalexpress.com. For coaches in Scotland, telephone Scottish Citylink on 08705 50 50 50 or visit: www.citylink.co.uk. For Northern Ireland, visit: www.translink.co.uk.

Usually, tickets for trains and underground systems such as the London Un- derground must be bought before you get on the train. The fare varies according to the day and time you wish to travel. Travelling in the rush hour is always more expensive. Discount tickets are available for families; people aged 60 and over, disabled people, students and people under 26. Ask at your local train station for details. Failure to buy a ticket may result in a penalty.

Taxis

To operate legally, all taxis and minicabs must be licensed and display a licence plate. Taxis and cabs with no licence are not insured for fare-paying passengers and are not always safe. Women should not use unlicensed minicabs.

Driving

You must be at least 17 to drive a car or motorcycle, 18 to drive a medium-sized lorry, and 21 to drive a large lorry or bus. To drive a lorry, minibus or bus with more than eight passenger seats, you must have a special licence.

The driving licence

You must have a driving licence to drive on public roads. To get a driving licence you must pass a test. There are many driving schools where you can learn with the help of a qualified instructor.

You get a full driving licence in three stages:

1. Apply for a provisional licence. You need this licence while you are learning to drive. With this you are allowed to drive a motorcycle up to 125cc or a car. You must put L plates on the vehicle, or D plates in Wales. Learner drivers cannot drive on a motorway. If you drive a car, you must be with someone who is over 21 and who has had a full licence for over three years. You can get an application form for a provisional licence from a post office.

2. Pass a written theory test

3. Pass a practical driving test

Drivers may use their licence until they are 70. After that the licence is valid for three years at a time.

In Northern Ireland, a newly-qualified driver must display an R-Plate (for registered driver) for one year after passing the test.

Overseas licences

If your driving licence is from a country in the European Union (EU), Iceland, Liechtenstein or Norway, you can drive in the UK for as long as your licence is valid.

If you have a licence from a country outside the EU), you may use it in the UK for up to 12 months. During this time you must get a UK provisional driving licence and pass both the UK theory and practical driving tests, or you will not be able to drive after 12 months.

Insurance

It is a criminal offence to have a car without proper motor insurance. Drivers without insurance can receive very high fines. It is also illegal to allow someone to use your car if they are not insured to drive it.

Road tax and MOT

You must also pay a tax to drive your car on the roads. This is called road tax. Your vehicle must have a road tax disc which shows you have paid. You can buy this at the post office. If you do not pay the road tax, your vehicle may be clamped or towed away.

If your vehicle is over three years old, you must take it every year for a Ministry of Transport (MOT) test. You can do this at an approved garage. The garage will give you an MOT certificate when your car passes the test. It is an offence not to have an MOT certificate. If you do not have an MOT certificate, your insurance will not be valid.

Safety

Everyone in a vehicle should wear a seat belt. Children under 12 years of age may need a special booster seat. Motorcyclists and their passengers must wear a crash helmet (this law does not apply to Sikh men if they are wearing a turban). It is illegal to drive while holding a mobile phone.

Speed limits

For cars and motorcycles the speed limits are:

30 miles per hour (mph) in built-up areas, unless a sign shows a different limit
60 mph on single carriageways
70 mph on motorways and dual carriageways

Speed limits are lower for buses, lorries and cars pulling caravans.

It is illegal to drive when you are over the alcohol limit or drunk. The police can stop you and give you a test to see how much alcohol you have in your body. This is called a breathalyser test. If a driver has more than the permitted amount of alcohol (called being 'over the limit') or refuses to take the test, he or she will be arrested. People who drink and drive can expect to be disqualified from driving for a long period.

Accidents

If you are involved in a road accident:

- don't drive away without stopping-this is a criminal offence
- call the police and ambulance on 999 or 112 if someone is injured
- get the names, addresses, vehicle registration numbers and insurance details of the other drivers
- give your details to the other drivers or passengers and to the police .
- make a note of everything that happened and contact your insurance company as soon as possible.

Note that if you admit the accident was your fault, the insurance company may refuse to pay. It is better to wait until the insurance company decides for itself whose fault the accident was.

Identity documents

At present, UK citizens do not have to carry identity (ID) cards. The government is, however, making plans to introduce them in the next few years.

Proving your identity

You may have to prove your identity at different times, such as when you open a bank account, rent accommodation, enrol for a college course, hire a car, apply for benefits such as housing benefit, or apply for a marriage certificate. Different organisations may ask for different documents as proof of identity. These can include:

- official documents from the Home Office showing your immigration status
- a certificate of identity
- a passport or travel document
- a National Insurance (NI) number card
- a provisional or full driving licence
- a recent gas, electricity or phone bill showing your name and address
- a rent or benefits book.

Check that you understand:

- How films are classified
- Why you need a television licence
- The rules about the selling and drinking of alcohol
- How to get a driving licence
- What you need to do to be allowed to drive a vehicle in the UK
- What you should do if you have an accident
- When you might have to prove your identity, and how you can do it

EMPLOYMENT

In this chapter there is information about:

- Looking for work and applying for jobs
- Training and volunteering
- Equal rights and discrimination
- Rights and responsibilities at work
- Working for yourself
- Childcare and children at work

Looking for work

If you are looking for work, or you are thinking of changing your job, there are a number of ways you can find out about work opportunities. The Home Office provides guidance on who is allowed to work in the UK. Not everyone in the UK is allowed to work and some people need work permits, so it is important to check your status before taking up work. Also, employers have to check that anyone they employ is legally entitled to work in the UK. For more information and guidance, see the Home Office website 'Working in the UK'- www.workingintheuk.gov.uk.

Jobs are usually advertised in local and national newspapers, at the local Jobcentre and in employment agencies. You can find the address and telephone number of your local Jobcentre under Jobcentre Plus in the phone book or see: www.jobcentreplus.gov.uk. Some jobs are advertised on supermarket notice boards and in shop windows. These jobs are usually part-time and the wages are often quite low. If there are particular companies you would like to work for, you can look for vacancies on their websites.

Jobcentre Plus is run by a government department-the Department for Work and Pensions. Trained staff gives advice and help in finding and applying for jobs as well claiming benefits. They can also arrange for interpreters. Their website www.jobcentreplus.gov.uk lists vacancies and training opportunities and gives general information on benefits. There is also a low cost telephone service-Jobseeker Direct, 0845 60 60 234. This is open 9 a.m. to 6 p.m. on weekdays and 9 a.m. to 1 p.m. on Saturdays.

Qualifications

Applicants for some jobs need special training or qualifications. If you have qualifications from another country, you can find out how they compare with qualifications in the UK at the National Academic Recognition Information Centre (NARIC), www.naric.org.uk.

For further information contact UK NARIC, ECCTIS Ltd, Oriel House, Oriel Road, Cheltenham Glos, GL50 1XP, telephone: 0870 990 4088, email: info@naric.org.uk.

Applications

Interviews for lower paid and local jobs can often be arranged by telephone or in person. For many jobs you need to fill in an application form or send a copy of your curriculum vitae (CV) with a covering letter or letter of application.

A covering letter is usually a short letter attached to a completed application form, while a letter of application gives more detailed information on why you are applying for the job and why you think you are suitable. Your CV gives specific details on your education, qualifications, previous employment, skills and interests. It is important to type any letters and your CV on a computer or word processor as this improves your chance of being called for an interview.

Employers often ask for the names and addresses of one or two referees. These are people such as your current or previous employer or college tutor. Referees need to know you well and to agree to write a short report or reference on your suitability for the job. Personal friends or members of your family are not normally acceptable as referees.

Interviews

In job descriptions and interviews, employers should give full details of what the job involves, including the pay, holidays and working conditions. If you need more information about any of these, you can ask questions in the interview. In fact, asking some questions in the interview shows you are interested and can improve your chance of getting the job.

When you are applying for a job and during the interview, it is important to be honest about your qualifications and experience. If an employer later finds out that you gave incorrect information, you might lose your job.

Criminal record

For some jobs, particularly if the work involves working with children or vulnerable people, the employer will ask for your permission to do a criminal record check. You can get more information on this from the Home Office Criminal Records Bureau (CRB) information line, telephone 0870 90 90 811. In Scotland, contact Disclosure Scotland: www.disclosurescotland.co.uk Helpline: 0870 609 6006.

Training

Taking up training helps people improve their qualifications for work. Some training may be offered at work or you can do courses from home or at your local college. This includes English language training. You can get more information from your local library and college or from websites such as www.worktrain.gov.uk and www.learndirect.co.uk. Learndirect offers a range of online training courses at centres across the country. There are charges for courses but you can do free starter or taster sessions. You can get more information from their free information and advice line: 0800 100 900.

Volunteering and work experience

Some people do voluntary work and this can be a good way to support your local community and organisations which depend on volunteers. It also provides useful experience that can help with future job applications. Your local library will have information about volunteering opportunities.

Check that you understand:

- The Home Office provides guidance on who is entitled to work in the UK
- NARIC can advise on how qualifications from overseas compare with qualifications from the UK
- What CVs are
- Who can be a referee
- What happens if any of the information you have given is untrue
- When you need a CRB check
- Where you can find out about training opportunities and job seeking
- Benefits of volunteering in terms of work experience and community involvement

Equal rights and discrimination

You can also get information and advice from websites such as: www.do-
.org.uk www.volunteering.org.uk and www.justdosomething.net. It is against
the law for employers to discriminate against someone at work. This means
that a person should not be refused work, training or promotion or treated less
favourably because of their:

- sex
- nationality, race, colour or ethnic group
- disability
- religion
- sexual orientation
- age

In Northern Ireland, the law also bans discrimination on grounds of religious
belief or political opinion.

The law also says that men and women who do the same job, or work of
equal value, should receive equal pay. Almost all the laws protecting people
at work apply equally to people doing part-time or full-time jobs.

There are, however, a small number of jobs where discrimination laws do not
apply. For example, discrimination is not against the law when the job involves
working for someone in their own home.

You can get more information about the law and racial discrimination from the
Commission for Racial Equality. The Equal Opportunities Commission can
help with sex discrimination issues and the Disability Rights Commission deals
with disability issues. Each of these organisations offers advice and information
and can, in some cases, support individuals. From October 2007 their functions
will be brought together in a new Commission for Equality and Human Rights.
You can get more information about the laws protecting people at work from
the Citizens Advice Bureau website: www.adviceguide.org.uk.

In Northern Ireland, the Equality Commission provides information and advice
in respect of all forms of unlawful discrimination.

The Commission for Racial Equality, St Dunstan's House,
201-211 Borough High Street, London, SE1 1GZ,
telephone: 020 7939 000, fax: 020 7939 0001, www.cre.gov.uk

The Equal Opportunities Commission, Arndale House, Arndale Centre,
Manchester M4 3EQ,
Telephone: 0845 601 5901, fax: 0161 838 8312, www.eoc.org.uk.

The Disability Rights Commission, DRC Helpline, FREEPOST M1D02164,
Stratford upon Avon CV37 9BR,
Telephone: 08457 622 633, fax: 08457 778 878, www.drc.org.uk.

The Equality Commission for Northern Ireland, Equality House,
7-9 Shaftesbury Square, Belfast BT2 7DP,
Telephone: 028 90 500600, www.equalityni.org.

Sexual harassment

Sexual harassment can take different forms. This includes:

- indecent remarks
- comments about the way you look that make you feel uncomfortable or humiliated
- comments or questions about your sex life
- inappropriate touching or sexual demands
- bullying behaviour or being treated in a way that is rude, hostile, degrading or humiliating because of your sex

Men and women can be victims of sexual harassment at work. If this happens to you, tell a friend, colleague or trade union representative and ask the person harassing you to stop. It is a good idea to keep a written record of what happened, the days and times when it happened and who else may have seen or heard the harassment. If the problem continues, report the person to your employer or trade union. Employers are responsible for the behaviour of their employees while they are at work. They should treat complaints of sexual harassment very seriously and take effective action to deal with the problem. If you are not satisfied with your employer's response, you can ask for advice and support from the Equal Opportunities Commission, your trade union or the Citizens Advice Bureau.

At work

Both employers and employees have legal responsibilities at work. Employers have to pay employees for the work that they do, treat them fairly and take responsible care for their health and safety. Employees should do their work with reasonable skill and care and follow all reasonable instructions. They should not damage their employer's business.

A written contract or statement

Within two months of starting a new job, your employer should give you a written contract or statement with all the details and conditions for your work. This should include your responsibilities, pay, working hours, holidays, sick pay and pension. It should also include the period of notice that both you and your employer should give for the employment to end. The contract or written statement is an important document and is very useful if there is ever a disagreement about your work, pay or conditions.

Pay, hours and holidays

Your pay is agreed between you and your employer. There is a minimum wage in the UK that is a legal right for every employed person above compulsory school leaving age. The compulsory school leaving age is 16, but the time in the school year when 16-year-olds can leave school in England and Wales is different from that in Scotland and Northern Ireland.

There are different minimum wage rates for different age groups. From October 2006 the rates are as follows:

- for workers aged 22 and above - £5.35 an hour
- for 18 -21 year olds - £4.45 an hour
- for 16 -17 year olds - £3.30 an hour.

Employers who pay their workers less than this are breaking the law. You can get more information from the Central Office of Information Directgov website, www.direct.gov.uk which has a wide range of public service information. Alternatively, you can telephone the National Minimum Wage Helpline, telephone: 0845 600 0678.

Your contract or statement will show the number of hours you are expected to work. Your employer might ask you if you can work more hours than this and it is your decision whether or not you do. Your employer cannot require you to work more hours than the hours agreed on your contract.

If you need to be absent from work, for example if you are ill or you have a medical appointment, it is important to tell your employer as soon as you can in advance. Most employees who are 16 or over are entitled to at least four weeks, paid holiday every year. This includes time for national holidays. Your employer must give you a pay slip, or a similar written statement, each time you are paid. This must show exactly how much money has been taken off for tax and national insurance contributions.

Tax

For most people, tax is automatically taken from their earnings by the employer and paid directly to HM Revenue and Customs, the government department responsible for collecting taxes. If you are self-employed, you need to pay your own tax. Money raised from income tax pays for government services such as roads, education, police and the armed forces. Occasionally HM Revenue and Customs sends out tax return forms which ask for full financial details. If you receive one, it is important to complete it and return the form as soon as possible. You can get help and advice from the HM Revenue and Customs self-assessment helpline, on: 0845 300 45 55.

National Insurance

Almost everybody in the UK who is in paid work, including self-employed people, must pay National Insurance (NI) contributions. Money raised from NI contributions is used to pay contributory benefits such as the State Retirement Pension and helps fund the National Health Service. Employees have their NI contributions deducted from their pay by their employer every week or month. People who are self-employed need to pay NI contributions themselves: Class 2 contributions, either by direct debit or every three months and Class 4 contributions on the profits from their trade or business. Class 4 contributions are paid alongside their income tax. Anyone who does not pay enough NI contributions will not be able to receive certain benefits, such as Jobseeker's Allowance or Maternity Pay, and may not receive a full state retirement pension.

Getting a National Insurance number

Just before their 16th birthday, all young people in the UK are sent a National Insurance number. This is a unique number for each person and it tracks their National Insurance contributions.

Refugees whose asylum applications have been successful have the same rights to work as any other UK citizen and to receive a National Insurance number. People who have applied for asylum and have not received a positive decision do not usually have permission to work and so do not get a National Insurance number.

You need a National Insurance number when you start work. If you do not have a National Insurance number, you can apply for one through Jobcentre Plus or your local Social Security Office. It is a good idea to make an appointment by telephone and ask which documents you need to take with you. You usually need to show your birth certificate, passport and Home Office documents allowing you to stay in the country. If you need information about registering for a National Insurance number, you can telephone the National Insurance Registrations Helpline on 0845 91 57006 or 0845 91 55670.

Pensions

Everyone in the UK who has paid enough National Insurance contributions will get a State Pension when they retire. The State Pension age for men is currently 65 years of age and for women it is 60, but the State Pension age for women will increase to 65 in stages between 2010 and 2020. You can find full details of the State Pension scheme on the State Pension website, www.thepensionservice.gov.uk or you can phone the Pension Service Helpline: 0845 60 60 265.

In addition to a State Pension, many people also receive a pension through their work and some also pay into a personal pension plan too. It is very important to get good advice about pensions. The Pensions Advisory Service gives free and confidential advice on occupational and personal pensions. Their helpline telephone number is 0845 601 2923 and their website address is www.opas.org.uk. Independent financial advisers can also give advice but you usually have to pay a fee for this service. You can find local financial advisers in the Yellow Pages and Thomson local guides or on the internet at www.unbiased.co.uk.

Health and safety

Employers have a legal duty to make sure the workplace is safe. Employees also have a legal duty to follow safety regulations and to work safely and responsibly. If you are worried about health and safety at your workplace, talk to your supervisor, manager or trade union representative. You need to follow the right procedures and your employer must not dismiss you or treat you unfairly for raising a concern.

Trade unions

Trade unions are organisations that aim to improve the pay and working conditions of their members. They also give their members advice and support on problems at work. You can choose whether to join a trade union or not and your employer cannot dismiss you or treat you unfairly for being a union member.

You can find details of trade unions in the UK, the benefits they offer to members and useful information on rights at work on the Trades Union Congress (TUC) website, www.tuc.org.uk.

Problems at work

If you have problems of any kind at work, speak to your supervisor, manager, trade union representative or someone else with responsibility as soon as possible. If you need to take any action, it is a good idea to get advice first. If you are a member of a trade union, your representative will help. You can also contact your local Citizens Advice Bureau (CAB) or Law Centre. The national Advisory, Conciliation and Arbitration Service (ACAS) website, www.acas.org.uk gives information on your rights at work. ACAS also offers a national helpline, telephone: 08457 47 47 47.

Losing your job and unfair dismissal

An employee can be dismissed immediately for serious misconduct at work. Anyone who cannot do their job properly, or is unacceptably late or absent from work, should be given a warning by their employer. If their work, punctuality or attendance does not improve, the employer can give them notice to leave their job.

It is against the law for employers to dismiss someone from work unfairly. If this happens to you, or life at work is made so difficult that you feel you have to leave, you may be able to get compensation if you take your case to an Employment Tribunal. This is a court which specialises in employment matters. You normally only have three months to make a complaint.

If you are dismissed from your job, it is important to get advice on your case as soon as possible. You can ask for advice and information on your legal rights and the best action to take from your trade union representative, a solicitor, a Law Centre or the Citizen's Advice Bureau.

Redundancy

If you lose your job because the company you work for no longer needs someone to do your job, or cannot afford to employ you, you may be entitled to redundancy pay. The amount of money you receive depends on the length of time you have been employed. Again your trade union representative, a solicitor, a Law Centre or the Citizens Advice Bureau can advise you.

Unemployment

Most people who become unemployed can claim Jobseeker's Allowance (JSA). This is currently available for men aged 18-65 and women aged 18-60 who are capable of working, available for work and trying to find work. Unemployed 16 and 17-year-olds may not be eligible for Jobseeker's Allowance but may be able to claim a Young Person's Bridging Allowance (YPBA) instead. The local Jobcentre Plus can help with claims. You can get further information from the Citizens Advice Bureau and the Jobcentre Plus website: www.jobcentreplus.gov.uk.

New Deal

New Deal is a government programme that aims to give unemployed people the help and support they need to get into work. Young people who have been unemployed for 6 months and adults who have been unemployed for 18 months are usually required to join New Deal if they wish to continue receiving benefit. There are different New Deal schemes for different age groups. You can find out more about New Deal on 0845 606 2626 or: www.newdeal.gov.uk.

The government also runs work-based learning programmes which offer training to people while they are at work. People receive a wage or an allowance and can attend college for one day a week to get a new qualification.

You can find out more about the different government schemes, and the schemes in your area, from Jobcentre Plus, www.jobcentreplus.gov.uk, or your local Citizens Advice Bureau.

Working for yourself

Tax

Self-employed people are responsible for paying their own tax and National Insurance. They have to keep detailed records of what they earn and spend on the business and send their business accounts to HM Revenue and Customs every year. Most self-employed people use an accountant to make sure they pay the correct tax and claim all the possible tax allowances.

As soon as you become self-employed you should register yourself for tax and National Insurance by ringing the HM Revenue and Customs telephone helpline for people who are self-employed, on 0845 915 4515.

Help and advice

Banks can give information and advice on setting up your own business and offer start-up loans, which need to be repaid with interest. Government grants and other financial support may be available. You can get details of these and advice on becoming self-employed from Business Link, a government-funded project for people starting or running a business- www.businesslink.gov.uk telephone: 0845 600 9 006.

Working in Europe

British citizens can work in any country that is a member of the European Economic Area (EEA). In general, they have the same employment rights as a citizen of that country or state.

Check that you understand:

Equal rights

- the categories covered by the law and exceptions
- equal job/equal pay regardless of gender
- the different commissions working to promote equal opportunities
- the grounds for sexual harassment complaints

At work

- the importance of contracts of employment
- the minimum wage and holiday entitlement
- information that has to be provided on pay slips

Tax

- what is deducted from your earnings and why
- the difference between being self-employed and employed
- where to get help if you need it when filling out forms
- the purpose of National Insurance and what happens if you don't pay enough contributions
- how you can get a National Insurance number

Pensions

- who is entitled to a pension
- what age men and women can get a pension

Health and safety

- employer and employee obligations
- what to do if you have concerns about health and safety

Trade unions

- what they are and who can join Losing your job

Losing your job

- where to go if you need advice on a problem at work
- possible reasons for dismissal
- the role of employment Tribunals
- who can help
- the timescale for complaining
- entitlement to redundancy pay

Self-employment

- responsibility for keeping detailed records and paying tax and national insurance
- the role of Business Link

Childcare and children at work

New mothers and fathers

Women who are expecting a baby have a legal right to time off work for ante-natal care. They are also entitled to at least 26 weeks' maternity leave. These rights apply to full-time and part-time workers and it makes no difference how long the woman has worked for her employer. It is, however, important to follow the correct procedures and to give the employer enough notice about taking maternity leave. Some women may also be entitled to maternity pay but this depends on how long they have been working for their employer.

Fathers who have worked for their employer for at least 26 weeks are entitled to paternity leave, which provides up to two weeks' time off from work, with pay, when the child is born. It is important to tell your employer well in advance.

You can get advice and more information on maternity and paternity matters from the personnel officer at work, your trade union representative, your local Citizens Advice Bureau, the Citizens Advice Bureau website www.adviceguide.org.uk or the government website www.direct.gov.uk

Childcare

It is Government policy to help people with childcare responsibilities to take up work. Some employers can help with this. The ChildcareLink website www.childcarelink.gov.uk gives information about different types of childcare and registered childminders in your area, or telephone 08000 96 02 96.

Hours and time for children at work

In the UK there are strict laws to protect children from exploitation and to make sure that work does not get in the way of their education. The earliest legal age for children to do paid work is set at 14. There are a few exceptions that allow children under the age of 14 to work legally and these include specific work in performing, modelling, sport and agriculture. In order to do any of this work, it is necessary to get a licence from the local authority.

By law, children aged 14 to 16 can only do light work. There are particular jobs they are not allowed to do and these include delivering milk, selling alcohol, cigarettes or medicines, working in a kitchen or a chip shop, working with dangerous machinery or doing any other kind of work that might cause them any kind of injury. Children who work have to get an employment card from their local authority and a medical certificate of fitness for work.

The law sets out clear limits for the working hours and times for 14-16 year-old children. Every child must have at least two consecutive weeks a year during the school holidays when they do not work. They cannot work:

- for more than 4 hours without a one-hour rest break
- for more than 2 hours on any school day or a Sunday
- before 7.a.m. or after 7.p.m.
- for more than one hour before school starts
- for more than 12 hours in any school week.

15 and 16-year-olds can work slightly more hours than 14-year-olds on a weekday when they are not at school, on Saturdays and in school holidays. The local authority has a duty to check that the law is obeyed. If it believes that a young person is working illegally, it can order that the young person is no longer employed. You can find more information on the TUC website, www.worksmart.org.uk.

Check that you understand:

Maternity and Paternity rights

- entitlement to maternity leave and pay for both part time and full time workers
- paternity leave entitlement
- the importance of following the right procedures and providing sufficient notice

Children at work

- minimum age for starting work
- jobs 14 to 16-year-year-olds are not allowed to do
- the maximum hours allowed
- requirements-medical certificate and employment card
- the local authority's responsibility for protecting children

Citizenship Practice Test

1. During the period 1880-1910; from which countries did the Jewish people migrate to the UK, in order to escape racist attacks (called 'pogroms')?
    a) Germany, France and Belgium
    b) France, Norway and Denmark
    c) Poland, Ukraine, Belarus
    d) Germany and Italy

2. Give two reasons why migrants came to the UK?
    a) Because they were forced to
    b) In the distant past, invaders came to Britain, seized land and stayed.
    c) To find safety, jobs and better life
    d) Because they had nowhere else to go

3. What kind of work did migrant Irish labourers do in the UK during the Irish famine?
    a) Work in textile mills
    b) Helped to build canals and railways across Britain
    c) Drove buses
    d) Teaching

4. Why did Huguenots (French Protestants) come to Britain?
    a) To escape from war
    b) To escape religious persecution
    c) To find employment
    d) To escape famine

5. Why did large numbers of Jewish people come to Britain during 1880 - 1910?
    a) To find employment
    b) To join the army
    c) To escape racist attacks they faced at home
    d) To escape the poverty they faced at home

6. Why did Irish migrants come to Britain during the mid 1840s?
    a) To escape famine in their country
    b) To invade and seize land
    c) To escape religious persecution
    d) To escape war

7. In which location did Britain set up bus driver recruitment centres, during the 1950's?
   a) India
   b) Ireland
   c) Pakistan
   d) West Indies

8. Where did textile and engineering firms from the north of England and the Midlands send agents to find workers?
   a) India and Pakistan
   b) West Indies
   c) Ireland
   d) America

9. What kind of work did the immigrants from Ireland and the West Indies do when they were invited into the UK after the Second World War?
   a) Help with farming
   b) Aid to reconstruction effort
   c) Join the army
   d) none of the above

10. In the 1980s who were not the largest immigrant groups to come to the United Kingdom?
    a) Americans
    b) Australians
    c) South Africans
    d) Indians

11. When did married women gain the right to retain ownership of their own money and property?
    a) 1982
    b) 1882
    c) 1782
    d) 1682

12. When did married women gain the right to divorce their husband?
    a) 1957
    b) 1945
    c) 1857
    d) 1757

13. When did women first gain the right to vote?
    a) 1818
    b) 1908
    c) 1918
    d) 1928

14. When did women get the same voting rights as men?
    a) 1818
    b) 1908
    c) 1918
    d) 1928

15. When women were first given the right to vote it was only permitted if they were
    a) 18 years or over
    b) 21 years or over
    c) 30 years or over
    d) 35 years or over

16. What percentage of the workforce is comprised of women?
    a) 30
    b) 40
    c) 45
    d) 50

17. Women in Britain today make up 51% of the population
    a) True
    b) False

18. Which gender group form the majority of students at the UK universities?
    a) Men
    b) Women
    c) Neither as numbers are equal
    d) Difficult to answer

19. Research shows that still many people today believe that women in Britain should stay at home and not go out to work.
    a) True
    b) False

20. What is the percentage of women with children (of school age), who also work?
   a) Almost 25%
   b) Almost 50%
   c) Almost 75%
   d) Almost 100%

21. What proportion of women with school age children are in paid employment?
   a) Almost quarter
   b) Almost half
   c) Almost three quarters
   d) Almost two thirds

22. On Average pay for women is about
   a) 10% lower than men
   b) 20% lower than men
   c) 30% lower than men
   d) 40% lower than men

23. Nearly half of all workforces in the UK are women.
   a) True
   b) False

24. Women still do not always have the same access to promotion and better-paid jobs than men.
   a) True
   b) False

25. After leaving university most women earn more than men.
   a) True
   b) False

26. Employment opportunities for women are much lower than in the past.
   a) True
   b) False

27. These days' girls leave school, on average, with better qualifications than boys.
   a) True
   b) False

28. How many young people (up to the age of 19) are there in the UK?
   a) 15 million
   b) 20 million
   c) 25million
   d) 30 million

29. What proportion of the UK population is made up of children and young people up to the age of 19?
   a) Almost three quarters
   b) Almost half
   c) Almost one quarter
   d) Almost 10 percent

30. What percentages of children live with both birth parents?
   a) 50%
   b) 60%
   c) 65%
   d) 70%

31. What percentage of children lives in single parent families?
   a) 10%
   b) 20%
   c) 25%
   d) 30%

32. What percentage of children lives with step families?
   a) 5%
   b) 10%
   c) 15%
   d) 20%

33. Almost a third of children in the UK live in a single parent family.
   a) True
   b) False

34. How often do most children in the UK receive their pocket money?
   a) Every day
   b) Every week
   c) Every month
   d) Not very often

35. Incidents of child molestation by strangers are increasing.
    a) True, there is evidence to suggest this
    b) False, there is no evidence to suggest this

36. Nowadays, children in the UK do not play outside the home as much as they did in the past. This is because,
    a) There is Home Entertainment
    b) They dislike active sports

37. The law states that children between the ages of 5 and 18 must attend school. Is this statement true or false?
    a) True
    b) False

38. In England and Scotland children take national tests in English, mathematics and science when they are
    a) 6, 7, 9 years old
    b) 7, 11, 14 years old
    c) 7, 9, 11 years old
    d) 7, 9, 14 years old

39. There is compulsory testing for children at ages 7, 11, and 14 in England and Scotland.
    a) True
    b) False

40. What does GCSE stand for?
    a) Generally Certified Simple Exam
    b) General Certificate of Secondary Education

41. When do most young people take their GCSE?
    a) When they are 16
    b) When they are 17
    c) When they are 18
    d) When they are 21

42. What is the GCSE equivalent in Scotland?
    a) Scottish Qualification Authority (SQA) Standard Grade
    b) Scottish Qualification Authority (SQA) Higher/Advanced Grade

43. AS levels are Advanced Subsidiary qualifications gained by completing six AS units. Is this statement true or false?
    a) True
    b) False

44. What does AGCE stand for?
    a) Advanced General Certification of Education
    b) Advanced General Certification Exam

45. How many AS units have to be studied to complete the AGCE qualification?
    a) 3
    b) 4
    c) 5
    d) 6

46. When do most young people take AS and A level exams?
    a) 15 and 16
    b) 16 and 17
    c) 17 and 18
    d) 18 and 21

47. Two in three young people now go on to higher education at college or university.
    a) True
    b) False

48. What percentage of young people now go on to higher education at college or university?
    a) 10%
    b) 33%
    c) 50%
    d) 66%

49. According to the law, which age group of children must attend school in England?
    a) 4 - 16
    b) 5 - 16
    c) 5 - 18
    d) 5 - 21

50. How do some people spend their gap year?
   a) Travelling overseas
   b) Earning money to pay for their university fees and living expenses
   c) Getting extra tuition
   d) Spending time with their parents .

51. How many children (under 18) are estimated to be working in the United Kingdom at any one time?
   a) 1 million
   b) 2 million
   c) 3 million
   d) 4 million

52. What are the most common jobs done by children under the age of 18?(Give 2 answers)
   a) Milk delivery
   b) In factories
   c) News paper delivery
   d) In supermarkets and newsagents

53. The employment of children is strictly controlled by law
   a) True
   b) False

54. Cigarette smoking among the adult population in Britain has risen significantly. Is this statement true or false?
   a) True
   b) False

55. More young people are smoking, and more girls smoke than boys. Is this statement true or false?
   a) True
   b) False

56. What is the minimum age for buying tobacco products?
   a) 15
   b) 16
   c) 17
   d) 18

57. In some areas, smoking in public buildings and work environments is not allowed.
   a) True
   b) False

58. What is the minimum age for buying alcohol?
   a) 15
   b) 16
   c) 18
   d) 21

59. What is meant by 'binge drinking'?
   a) Consuming large amounts of alcohol within a short period of time
   b) Consuming small amounts of alcohol over a long period of time

60. Which of these drugs are illegal to posses?
   a) Heroin
   b) Cocaine
   c) Cannabis
   d) All of the above

61. Cocaine is illegal to
   a) Produce
   b) Possess
   c) Supply
   d) All of the above

62. According to statistics, half of all young adults, and about a third of the population as a whole, have used illegal drugs at one time or the other.
   a) True
   b) False

63. There is a strong link between the use of hard drugs and crime. Is this statement true or false?
   a) True
   b) False

64. There is no link between the use of hard drugs and mental illness. Is this statement true or false?
   a) True
   b) False

65. Young people in Britain can vote in elections from the age of
    a) 16
    b) 18
    c) 21
    d) 30

66. What is the proportion of first time voters who used their vote in the 2001 general election?
    a) 1 in 5
    b) 2 in 5
    c) Nearly half
    d) None

67. What is the percentage of first time voters who used their vote in the 2001 general election?
    a) 10
    b) 20
    c) 30
    d) 50

68. According to a survey carried out in 2003 among young people, what were some of the most important issues in Britain?(Give 3 answers)
    a) War/terrorism
    b) Drugs
    c) Racism
    d) Unemployment

69. According to a survey 86% of young people have taken part in some form of community event over the past year.
    a) True
    b) False

70. What was the population of the United Kingdom in 2005?
    a) 50.1 million
    b) 5.1 million
    c) 2.9 million
    d) 59.8 million

71. The UK population has grown by 7.7% since 1971?
    a) True
    b) False

72. Since 1971 the United Kingdom's population has grown by
    a) 17%
    b) 10%
    c) 7.7%
    d) 5.1%

73. Over the last 20 years, there has been a decline in the population in the North East and North West of England. Is this statement true or false?
    a) True
    b) False

74. The United Kingdom has an aging population and has a record number of people aged 85 and over. Is this statement true or false?
    a) True
    b) False

75. Why does the United Kingdom have an ageing population?
    a) Because the birth rate and the death rate are increasing.
    b) Because the birth rate and the death rate are falling.

76. There are less people over 60 than children under 16. Is this statement true or false?
    a) True
    b) False

77. What is the population of England?
    a) 50.1 million
    b) 5.1 million
    c) 2.9 million
    d) 1.7 million

78. What is the population of Scotland?
    a) 50.1 million
    b) 5.1 million
    c) 2.9 million
    d) 1.7 million

79. What is the population of Wales?
    a) 50.1 million
    b) 5.1 million
    c) 2.9 million
    d) 1.7 million

80. What is the population of Northern Ireland?
    a) 50.1 million
    b) 5.1 million
    c) 2.9 million
    d) 1.7 million

81. What percentage of the UK population lives in England?
    a) 84%
    b) 8%
    c) 5%
    d) 3%

82. What percentage of the UK population lives in Scotland?
    a) 84%
    b) 8%
    c) 5%
    d) 3%

83. What percentage of the UK population lives in Wales?
    a) 84%
    b) 8%
    c) 5%
    d) 3%

84. What percentage of the UK population lives in Northern Ireland?
    a) 84%
    b) 8%
    c) 5%
    d) 3%

85. Which country in the UK has the largest population?
    a) England
    b) Scotland
    c) Wales
    d) Northern Ireland

86. Which country in the UK has the second largest population?
    a) England
    b) Scotland
    c) Wales
    d) Northern Ireland

87. Some of the statistics collected on census forms are(select more than one)
    a) Ethnicity
    b) Place of birth
    c) Physical appearance
    d) Health

88. When was the first census carried out in the United Kingdom?
    a) 1701
    b) 1801
    c) 1901
    d) 1941

89. When will the next UK census be carried out?
    a) 2008
    b) 2009
    c) 2010
    d) 2011

90. How often is a full census carried out in the United Kingdom?
    a) every 3 years
    b) every 5 years
    c) every 6 years
    d) every 10 years

91. Why was the 1941 census not carried out in the United Kingdom?
    a) There was not enough time to carry out the full census
    b) The Second World War was in progress
    c) The government did not plan a census
    d) Not enough people were willing to participate

92. How many years must have passed before an individual's census form is viewable by the general public?
    a) 10
    b) 50
    c) 90
    d) 100

93. How is general census information used?
    a) To keep a check on migration
    b) To identify population trends
    c) To help with planning future needs
    d) Not used at all

94. What percentage does people of Indian, Pakistan, Chinese, Black Caribbean, Black African, Bangladeshi and mixed ethnic descent make up the UK population?
    a) 10.2%
    b) 8.3%
    c) 7.7%
    d) 6.3%

95. Today about half of Indian, Pakistan, Chinese, Black Caribbean, Black African, Bangladeshi and mixed ethnic descent communities were born in the United Kingdom. Is this statement true or false?
    a) True
    b) False

96. What percentage of the UK's population is white?
    a) 100%
    b) 92%
    c) 88%
    d) 80%

97. What is the largest ethnic minority in Britain?
    a) Indian
    b) Pakistani
    c) Bangladeshi
    d) Black Caribbean

98. Most members of the large ethnic minority groups in the UK live in England. Is this statement true or false?
    a) True
    b) False

99. What percentages of the UK's ethnic minorities live in the London area?
    a) 27%
    b) 39%
    c) 45%
    d) 51%

100. What percentage of England's population is made up of ethnic minorities?
 a) 45%
 b) 39%
 c) 9%
 d) 8.3%

101. What percentage of London's population is made up of ethnic minorities?
 a) 45%
 b) 39%
 c) 29%
 d) 9%

102. Nearly two-third of the population in London is ethnic minorities. Is this statement true or false?
 a) True
 b) False

103. 2 % of Scotland's population are ethnic minorities
 a) True
 b) False

104. What percentage of Wales's population is made up of ethnic minorities?
 a) 9%
 b) 7%
 c) 5%
 d) 2%

105. What is the distance from the north coast of Scotland to the south west coast of England?
 a) Approx 1000 km
 b) Approx 1400 km
 c) Approx 500 km
 d) Approx 250km

106. Where is the Cockney dialect spoken?
 a) Tyneside
 b) Liverpool
 c) London
 d) Scotland

107. Where is the Geordie dialect spoken?
    a) Tyneside
    b) Liverpool
    c) London
    d) Scotland

108. Where is the Scouse dialect spoken?
    a) Tyneside
    b) Liverpool
    c) London
    d) Scotland

109. Where is the Gaelic language spoken?
    a) Tyneside
    b) Liverpool
    c) London
    d) Highlands and Islands of Scotland and in Northern Ireland.

110. Where is the Welsh language spoken?
    a) Tyneside
    b) Scotland
    c) Wales
    d) Liverpool

111. According to the 2001 Census, what percentage of people stated that they were Christian?
    a) 99.0%
    b) 90.0%
    c) 71.6%
    d) 66.6%

112. According to the 2001 Census, what percentage of people stated that they were Roman Catholic?
    a) 5%
    b) 10%
    c) 15%
    d) 20%

113. According to the 2001 Census what percentage of people stated that they were Muslim?
    a) 1.1%
    b) 2.7%
    c) 3.1%
    d) 4.0%

114. According to the 2001 Census, what percentage of people stated that they had a religion?
    a) 95%
    b) 85%
    c) 75%
    d) 65%

115. According to the 2001 Census, what percentage of people stated that they had no religion?
    a) 10.0%
    b) 20.0%
    c) 25.0%
    d) 15.5%

116. According to the 2001 Census, what percentage of people stated that they were Hindus?
    a) 1.0%
    b) 2.0%
    c) 3.0%
    d) 4.0%

117. According to the 2001 Census, what percentage of people stated that they were Sikh?
    a) 1.0%
    b) 0.6%
    c) 0.5%
    d) 0.1%

118. According to the 2001 Census, what percentage of people stated that they were Jewish?
    a) 1.0%
    b) 0.6%
    c) 0.5%
    d) 0.1%

119. According to the 2001 Census, what percentage of people stated that they were Buddhist?
    a) 1.0%
    b) 0.6%
    c) 0.5%
    d) 0.3%

120. The Church of England is also known as The Anglican Church in other countries?
    a) True
    b) False

121. The Church of England is also known as
    a) The Kirk
    b) The Anglican Church
    c) The Vatican
    d) The Presbyterian Church

122. When did Church of England come into existence?
    a) in the 1530s
    b) in the 1630s
    c) in the 1710s
    d) in the 1830s

123. Who is the head of the Church of England?
    a) The king or queen
    b) The Archbishop of Canterbury
    c) The Prime Minister
    d) The Chancellor of the Exchequer

124. Who is the Supreme Governor of the Church of England?
    a) The king or queen
    b) The Archbishop of Canterbury
    c) The Prime Minister
    d) The Chancellor of the Exchequer

125. Who is the spiritual leader of the Church of England?
    a) The king or queen
    b) The Archbishop of Canterbury
    c) The Prime Minister
    d) The Chancellor of the Exchequer

126. The Archbishop of Canterbury is selected by
   a) Prime Minister and a committee appointed by the church
   b) The Queen

127. The Monarch is not allowed to marry
   a) Muslim
   b) Hindu
   c) Catholic
   d) All of the above

128. The Monarch is only allowed to marry
   a) Catholic
   b) Protestant
   c) Muslim
   d) Christian

129. What is the established church in Scotland?
   a) The Anglican church
   b) The Presbyterian Church
   c) The Vatican
   d) There is no established Church in Scotland

130. Who is the head of the Presbyterian Church in Scotland?
   a) The Chief Moderator
   b) The Archbishop of Canterbury
   c) The king or queen
   d) Chief Minister of Scotland

131. Who has the right to select the Archbishop of Canterbury?
   a) The Prime Minister
   b) The king or the queen
   c) The outgoing Archbishop of Canterbury
   d) The public

132. What is the established church in Wales?
   a) The Church of England
   b) The Presbyterian Church
   c) The Anglican church
   d) There is no established church in Wales

133. What is the established church in Northern Ireland?
    a) The Church of England
    b) The Presbyterian Church
    c) The Anglican church
    d) There is no established church in Northern Ireland

134. Name some of the Protestant Christian groups in the UK (select more than one)
    a) Baptists
    b) Methodists
    c) Hanukkahs
    d) Quakers

135. According to estimates what percentage of England's population regularly attends religious services?
    a) 5%
    b) 10%
    c) 15%
    d) 20%

136. Who is the patron saint of England?
    a) St David
    b) St Patrick
    c) St George
    d) St Andrew

137. Who is the patron saint of Wales?
    a) St David
    b) St Patrick
    c) St George
    d) St Andrew

138. Who is the patron saint of Scotland?
    a) St David
    b) St Patrick
    c) St George
    d) St Andrew

139. Who is the patron saint of Northern Ireland?
    a) St David
    b) St Patrick
    c) St George
    d) St Andrew

140. Which national day is celebrated with a holiday?
    a) St David's day
    b) St Patrick's day
    c) St George's day
    d) St Andrew's day

141. Name the country in the UK where St Andrew's Day is celebrated on the 30th of November?
    a) England
    b) Scotland
    c) Wales
    d) Northern Ireland

142. Name the country in the UK where St George's Day is celebrated on the 23rd of April?
    a) England
    b) Scotland
    c) Wales
    d) Northern Ireland

143. Name the country in the UK where St Patrick's Day is celebrated on the 17th of March?
    a) England
    b) Scotland
    c) Wales
    d) Northern Ireland

144. Name the country in the UK where St David's Day is celebrated on the 1st of March?
    a) England
    b) Scotland
    c) Wales
    d) Northern Ireland

145. Which country in the United Kingdom celebrates its national day with a public holiday?
    a) England
    b) Scotland
    c) Wales
    d) Northern Ireland

146. In which order do the UK national days fall?
   a) St Patrick's Day, St George's Day, St David's Day, St Andrew's Day
   b) St George's Day, St David's Day, St Patrick's Day, St Andrew's Day
   c) St David's Day, St Andrew's Day, St Patrick's Day, St George's Day
   d) St David's Day, St Patrick's Day, St George's Day, St Andrew's Day

147. When is St George's day celebrated?
   a) 1STMarch
   b) 17th March
   c) 23rd April
   d) 30th November

148. When is St Patrick's Day celebrated?
   a) 1STMarch
   b) 17th March
   c) 23rd April
   d) 30th November

149. When is St David's day celebrated?
   a) 1STMarch
   b) 17th March
   c) 23rd April
   d) 30th November

150. When is St Andrew's day celebrated?
   a) 1STMarch
   b) 17th March
   c) 23rd April
   d) 30th November

151. How many Bank Holidays are there in the UK?
   a) 4
   b) 5
   c) 7
   d) 9

152. Name the main Christian festivals celebrated in the UK
   a) New Year
   b) Christmas and Easter
   c) Hanukkah
   d) Eid ul-Fitr

153. Name the main Muslim festival celebrated in the UK
a) Diwali
b) Christmas and Easter
c) Hanukkah
d) Eid ul-Fitr

154. Name the main Hindu festival celebrated in the UK
a) Diwali
b) Christmas and Easter
c) Hanukkah
d) Eid ul-Fitr

155. Name the main Jewish festival celebrated in the UK
a) Diwali
b) Christmas and Easter
c) Hanukkah
d) Eid ul-Fitr

156. Give 2 examples of festivals of art, music and culture celebrated in the UK
a) The Notting Hill Carnival
b) Hanukkah
c) The Edinburgh Festival
d) The New Year

157. When is Christmas celebrated?
a) 24th of December
b) 25th of December
c) 26th of December
d) 31st of December

158. What does Christmas day celebrates?
a) The birth of Jesus Christ
b) The death of Jesus Christ
c) Beginning of a new year
d) End of a year

159. Two traditional dishes eaten on Christmas Day are
a) Fish and chips
b) Turkey
c) Christmas pudding
d) Easter eggs

160. How is Christmas celebrated in the UK? (give more than 1 answer)
    a) By giving each other gifts
    b) By decorating their houses
    c) By dressing up as turkeys
    d) By giving each other cards

161. How do the very young children believe they get their Christmas presents?
    a) Parents buy it for them
    b) Father Christmas (or Santa Claus) brings them during the night
    c) They get by them magic
    d) They are not sure

162. How is Father Christmas described in pictures?
    a) Having a short beard
    b) Having a long beard and dressed in red
    c) Having a long beard and dressed in black
    d) Having a short beard and dressed in winter clothes

163. When is Boxing Day celebrated?
    a) 24th of December
    b) 25th of December
    c) 26th of December
    d) 31st of December

164. Is Boxing Day a public holiday?
    a) Yes
    b) No

165. When is the New Year celebrated in the United Kingdom?
    a) 25 December
    b) 26 December
    c) 1 January
    d) 2 January

166. Is New Year a public holiday?
    a) Yes
    b) No

167. What is the 31st December called in Scotland?
    a) New Year
    b) New Years eve
    c) Hogmanay
    d) Boxing day

168. The 2nd January is also a holiday in Scotland. Is this statement true or false?
    a) True
    b) False

169. Which of these statements about Hogmanay is true?
    a) In Scotland Hogmanay is a bigger holiday for some people than Christmas
    b) In Scotland Hogmanay is not very well known.

170. When is Valentine's Day?
    a) 25th December
    b) 1st January
    c) 14th February
    d) 1st April

171. What traditionally happens on St Valentine's Day?
    a) Boyfriends and girlfriends exchange cards and presents
    b) Husband and wives exchange cards and presents
    c) Secret admirers gives unsigned cards
    d) Traditionally all of the above happen

172. What traditionally happens on April's Fools day? (Give 2 answers)
    a) People play jokes on each other
    b) Some TV and newspapers carry stories intended to deceive credulous viewers and readers
    c) People give each other cards and gifts
    d) Public holiday

173. When is Mothering Sunday?
    a) 1 week before Easter
    b) 2 weeks before Easter
    c) 3 weeks before Easter
    d) 4 weeks before Easter

174. What traditionally happens on Mothering Sunday?
    a) Mothers get a public holiday
    b) Children send cards or buy gifts for their mothers

175. What does Easter commemorate?
    a) The birth of Jesus Christ
    b) The resurrection of Jesus Christ

176. When is Halloween?
    a) First week in April
    b) 5th November
    c) 31st October
    d) 11th November

177. Which of these statements is correct about Halloween?
    a) People set off fireworks displays
    b) Young people usually dress up in frightening costumes to play 'trick or treat'

178. In which festival do people carry lanterns made out of pumpkins with candles inside?
    a) Valentine's Day
    b) Mother's Day
    c) Halloween
    d) Guy Fawkes Night

179. When is Guy Fawkes Night?
    a) 1st April
    b) 31st October
    c) 5th November
    d) 11th November

180. What does Guy Fawkes Night commemorate?
    a) People who died in The First World War
    b) People who died in The Second World War
    c) A failed attempt by Guy Fawkes and his group to kill the king with a bomb in the Houses of Parliament
    d) Creation of fireworks displays

181. Which of these statements is correct about Guy Fawkes Night?
    a) On that day, people in Britain cook special meals and invite their friends over.
    b) On that day, people in Britain set off fireworks at home or in special displays.

182. When is Remembrance Day celebrated?
    a) 31 October
    b) 5 November
    c) 14 February
    d) 11 November

183. Remembrance Day celebrates the victories of World Wars. (True or False)?
    a) True
    b) False

184. Which of these statements is true about Remembrance Day?
    a) Many people wear poppies in memory of those who died in World Wars and other wars.
    b) Many people set off fire works to celebrate the victories of World Wars.

185. Select two correct statements about Remembrance Day
    a) Many people wear poppies
    b) There is a two minutes silence observed at 11 a.m.
    c) Fire works are set off in the night
    d) People play trick or treat.

186. Which of the sports listed below have a large following (select more than one)?
    a) Football
    b) Cricket
    c) Bowling
    d) Rugby

187. From the list below which can be considered a major sporting event?
    a) FA cup final
    b) Wimbledon tennis championships
    c) Grand National horse race
    d) All of the above

188. What is the Grand National?
    a) Football tournament
    b) Horse race
    c) Tennis tournament
    d) Cricket tournament

189. What does FA stand for?
    a) Family Association
    b) Fancy dress Association
    c) Footballers Anonymous
    d) Football Association

190. What is the name of the popular UK tennis tournament played in South London?
    a) Grand National
    b) FA cup
    c) Wimbledon tennis tournament
    d) Bowling

191. There are no United Kingdom teams for football and rugby. Is this statement true or false?
    a) True
    b) False

192. United Kingdom's constitution is written by
    a) The Queen
    b) The Archbishop of Canterbury
    c) No one. It is an unwritten constitution
    d) Parliament

193. Who is the Head of State of the United Kingdom?
    a) The Prime Minister
    b) Queen Elizabeth II
    c) Queen Elizabeth I
    d) Home Secretary

194. Who is the current heir to the throne?
    a) Prince Charles
    b) Princess Ann
    c) Prince Philip
    d) Prince William

195. United Kingdom has a constitutional monarchy. Is this statement true or false?
   a) True
   b) False

196. Which of the following countries have a constitutional monarchy? (give more than one answer)
   a) Norway
   b) Spain
   c) Sweden
   d) United States of America

197. What is meant by constitutional monarchy?
   a) King or queen rule the country
   b) King or queen does not rule the country, but appoints the government which the people have chosen in democratic elections.

198. When did Queen Elizabeth II start her reign?
   a) 1900
   b) 1942
   c) 1952
   d) 1962

199. The Queen is allowed to criticise or support the government publicly on certain issues. Is this statement true or false?
   a) True
   b) False

200. The Queen's Speech is provided by the
   a) The speaker of the House of Commons
   b) The Prime Minister

201. What does the Queen's speech contain?
   a) The government's policies for the year ahead
   b) A speech written by the Queen

202. Select one of the important ceremonial roles performed by the Queen.
   a) The opening of the new parliamentary session each year
   b) Attending Ascot

203. What famous phrase describes the level of expression that the monarch is restricted to when discussing government matters?
    a) Encourage, advise and observe
    b) Advise, warn and encourage
    c) Overrule, argue and advise
    d) Warn, revise and observe

204. Members of the House of Lords may stand for election to the House of Commons. Is this statement true or false?
    a) True
    b) False

205. The general elections are held in the UK
    a) At least every year
    b) At least every 3 years
    c) At least every 5 years
    d) At least every 6 years

206. How many constituencies are there in the United Kingdom?
    a) 108
    b) 129
    c) 646
    d) 500

207. Where is the House of Commons situated?
    a) Buckingham Palace
    b) Windsor Castle
    c) The Palace of Westminster
    d) No 10 Downing Street

208. What does MP stand for?
    a) Prime Minister
    b) Member of Parliament
    c) Man of the People
    d) Minister of Parliament

209. What are the Responsibilities of an MP?
    a) Representing their constituency
    b) Helping to create and shape new laws
    c) Scrutinising and comment on what the government is doing
    d) All of the above

210. How many MPs are there in the United Kingdom Parliament?
   a) 109
   b) 129
   c) 646
   d) 500

211. Can a general election be held earlier than a 5 year period?
   a) No, the law states that it should be held every 5 years.
   b) Yes, if the Prime Minister so decides.

212. UK MPs are elected on the basis of
   a) Proportional Representation
   b) First past the post system

213. Give two reasons, why by-elections are held?
   a) When an MP resign
   b) When an MP Dies
   c) When the Prime Minister feels like it
   d) When the Queen wishes

214. In an election, what is meant by first past the post system?
   a) A candidate in a constituency who gains more votes than any other is elected
   b) A candidate in a constituency who gains the majority of the total votes cast is elected

215. Can a party candidate win a constituency if they don't get the majority of votes?
   a) Yes
   b) No

216. The government is formed by
   a) The party which wins the majority of constituencies
   b) The party with the second largest number of MPs in the House Of Commons
   c) The Party favoured by the Queen
   d) The Party which won the largest number of votes

217. What is the name of a small group of MPs who ensure the discipline and attendance of MPs at voting time in the House of Commons?
    a) seniors
    b) Whips
    c) Ministers
    d) Secretaries of state

218. How are Whips appointed?
    a) By the Prime Minister
    b) By the King or Queen
    c) By the Speaker
    d) By their party leaders

219. In which elections is Proportional Representation used? (give 3 answers)
    a) European Parliament elections
    b) Scottish Parliament elections
    c) English Parliament elections
    d) Welsh Assembly

220. What are whips responsible for? (Give 2 answers)
    a) Make sure MPs gets paid
    b) Discipline in their party
    c) Making sure MPs attend the House of Commons to vote
    d) Making government policies

221. Elections for the European Parliament are held
    a) Every 3 years
    b) Every 5 years
    c) Every 6 years
    d) Every year

222. How many representatives from the UK are there in the European Parliament?
    a) 109
    b) 129
    c) 646
    d) 78

223. What does MEP stand for?
    a) Member of the European Parliament
    b) Member of Elected Person

224. Members of European Parliament are elected on the basis of
    a) First past the post system
    b) Proportional representation

225. In an election, what is meant by proportional representation?
    a) A candidate in a constituency who gains the majority of the total votes cast is elected.
    b) Whereby seats are allocated to each party in proportion to the total votes it won.

226. In what year did the Prime Minister gain the power to be able to appoint members of the House of Lords?
    a) 1938
    b) 1948
    c) 1958
    d) 1968

227. A member of the House of Lords appointed by the Prime Minister is called
    a) Quango
    b) Life Peer
    c) Hereditary Peer
    d) Member of Lords

228. Life Peers have to be Christians
    a) True no other faith members are allowed
    b) False, other faith members can also be life peers

229. What is the main role of the House of Lords?
    a) Refuse to allow laws proposed by the House of Commons
    b) Agree with all the laws propose by the House of Commons
    c) Examine in detail, the new laws proposed by the House of Commons and suggest amendments or changes
    d) Gather once a week

230. What was the only way the members could be appointed to the House of Lords in the past? (give 2 answers)
    a) By being peers of the realm (hereditary aristocrats)
    b) By doing favours to the king or queen
    c) By standing in elections
    d) Senior judges, or bishops of the Church of England

231. Can all hereditary peers attend the House of Lords?
    a) Yes. They all have the general right to attend the House of Lords
    b) No. Only the elected members can attend
    c) No. Only the Life Peers can attend
    d) No. They must first get approval from the Prime Minister.

232. Which of these statements about the House of Lords is correct?
    a) The House of Lords can only delay the passage of new laws
    b) The House of Lords may reject laws proposed by the House of Commons

233. The House of Commons has powers to overrule the House of Lords. Is this statement true or false?
    a) True
    b) False

234. How are Life Peers appointed?
    a) Life Peers are appointed by the Queen on the advice of the Prime Minister.
    b) Life Peers are appointed by the Prime Minister.

235. The Prime Minister is
    a) The leader of the political party in power
    b) The leader of the opposition party

236. The Prime Minister
    a) Can not appoint (or dismiss) members of the Cabinet.
    b) Can appoint (or dismiss) members of the Cabinet.

237. The Prime Minister's official residence is
    a) Palace of Westminster
    b) No 10 Downing Street
    c) Buckingham Palace
    d) No 11 Downing Street

238. What is the Prime Ministers country house called?
    a) Buckingham Palace
    b) Palace of Westminster
    c) Chequers
    d) Stormont

239. The Prime Minister can be changed by (Give 2 answers)
    a) The Queen
    b) If he or she wishes to resign
    c) Archbishop of Canterbury
    d) The Party to which he or she belongs

240. How is the Prime Minister appointed?
    a) By the Queen
    b) By the parliament
    c) By being the leader of the Party that form the Government
    d) By winning the Prime Ministerial election held at the same time as the Parliamentary election

241. Who resides at no 10 Downing Street?
    a) The Queen
    b) The Prime Minister
    c) The Chancellor of the Exchequer
    d) The Lord Chancellor

242. What is the role of the Prime Minister? (Give 2 answers)
    a) Appoints (and dismisses) members of the Cabinet and other public positions
    b) Head of State
    c) Leader of the party in power
    d) Speaker of the House of Commons

243. The Cabinet consists of
    a) Opposition MPs
    b) About 20 senior MPs

244. How often does the cabinet meet?
    a) Every Day
    b) Once a week
    c) Twice a week
    d) Once a month

245. What happens to policy and law decisions once they have been agreed by cabinet?
    a) They are submitted to Parliament for approval
    b) They are submitted to The Queen for approval
    c) They are submitted to The House of Lords for approval
    d) They are made into laws

246. What is the title of the minister who is responsible for the economy?
    a) The Home Secretary
    b) The Foreign Secretary
    c) The chancellor of the Exchequer
    d) The Lord Chancellor

247. What is the title of the minister who is responsible for law and order and immigration?
    a) The Home Secretary
    b) The Foreign Secretary
    c) The chancellor of the Exchequer
    d) The Lord Chancellor

248. What is the title of the minister who is responsible for foreign affairs?
    a) The Home Secretary
    b) The Foreign Secretary
    c) The chancellor of the Exchequer
    d) The Lord Chancellor

249. What is the title of the minister who is responsible for legal affairs?
    a) The Home Secretary
    b) The Foreign Secretary
    c) The chancellor of the Exchequer
    d) The Lord Chancellor

250. How are ministers of state appointed?
    a) By the Prime Minister
    b) By the Queen
    c) Selected by the Parliament
    d) Voted by the party they belong to.

251. Since when was the Lord Chancellor allowed to sit in the Commons?
    a) 1958
    b) 1997
    c) 1999
    d) 2005

252. The second largest party in the House of Commons is referred to as
    a) Her Majesty's Government
    b) Her Majesty's Loyal Opposition
    c) Her Majesty's Party
    d) Shadow Party

253. When can Members of Parliament ask question of Government Ministers?
   a) During cabinet meetings
   b) During Question Time

254. What is Prime Ministers Question time?
   a) Its when members of the public ask questions of the Prime Minister
   b) Its when Members of Parliament ask questions of the Prime Minister

255. The Opposition has a guaranteed amount of time to debate issues it chooses. Is this statement true or false?
   a) True
   b) False

256. What is the shadow cabinet?
   a) Senior members of the main opposition party who lead criticism of Government Ministers
   b) Senior members of the Government who resign from the cabinet

257. Who is the Speaker of the House of Commons?
   a) An MP
   b) A person appointed by the Queen
   c) A person appointed by the Prime Minister
   d) Heir to the throne

258. How is the Speaker of the House of Commons chosen?
   a) He is appointed by the Prime Minister
   b) He is appointed by the Queen
   c) He is elected by fellow MPs
   d) He is chosen by the Lords

259. What is the role of the Speaker in the House of Commons? (Give 2 answers)
   a) Defends the rights of the Queen in Parliament
   b) Defends the debating rights of the Opposition in Parliament
   c) Defends the right of the ruling Party
   d) Chairs the proceedings in the House of Commons

260. You have to belong to a political party if you want to stand for election. Is this statement true or false?
   a) True
   b) False

261. MPs who do not represent any of the main political parties are called
    a) Independents
    b) Supporters

262. How often is policy making conferences held by political parties?
    a) Every few years
    b) Every year
    c) Twice a year
    d) Every five years

263. What is meant by pressure groups?
    a) Selection of MPs in the cabinet
    b) Opposition MPs
    c) Organisations that try to influence Government policý.
    d) Government organisations

264. Ordinary citizens today are more likely to support pressure groups than join a political party. Is this statement true or false?
    a) True
    b) False

265. What is the name of an independent manager or administrator who has a job requiring them to carry out Government policy?
    a) Quango
    b) Pressure group
    c) Civil servants
    d) Temps

266. What are the two key features of the civil service?
    a) Neutrality
    b) Favouritism
    c) Efficiency
    d) Professionalism

267. What are civil servants?
    a) They are managers and administrators who carry out government policy
    b) Appointed by government to carry out their policy

268. Which country in the UK does not have its own parliament or national assembly?
   a) England
   b) Scotland
   c) Wales
   d) Northern Ireland

269. When did the government started a programme of devolved adminis- tration for Wales and Scotland?
   a) 1922
   b) 1977
   c) 1997
   d) 1999

270. In which year was the Assembly for Wales and the Scottish Parliament created?
   a) 1922
   b) 1997
   c) 1999
   d) 2001

271. What are the three areas of policy which always remain under the control of the central UK government?
   a) Defence
   b) Foreign affairs
   c) Housing and education
   d) Taxation

272. Scottish Parliament and Welsh assembly were both set up using forms of proportional representation to ensure
   a) Single party always wins an election
   b) They were not dominated by a single party

273. Proportional representation for elections to the Northern Ireland as- sembly was introduced to ensure
   a) Unionist majority takes all the posts in the government
   b) Power sharing between Unionist and Irish Nationalist

274. Where is the Welsh Assembly Government for Wales situated?
    a) Cardiff
    b) Glasgow
    c) London
    d) Stormont

275. How many Assembly Members (AM) are there in the Welsh Assembly Government for Wales?
    a) 50
    b) 60
    c) 108
    d) 129

276. Assembly Members of the Welsh Assembly Government for Wales can only speak in Welsh. Is this statement true or false?
    a) True
    b) False

277. Give 3 examples of matters on which the Welsh Assembly Government can legislate
    a) Education policy
    b) Environment
    c) Foreign policy
    d) Transport

278. The Welsh assembly can pass laws for Wales on anything not specifically reserved for Westminster
    a) Yes. Within a statutory framework set out by the UK Parliament at Westminster
    b) No. They are not allowed to pass any laws.

279. Where is the Parliament of Scotland situated?
    a) London
    b) Cardiff
    c) Edinburgh
    d) Stormont

280. How many members are there in the Scottish Parliament?
    a) 646
    b) 60
    c) 129
    d) 108

281. The Scottish Parliament can pass legislation on anything not specifically reserved for Westminster. Is this statement true or false?
    a) True
    b) False

282. Give 3 examples of matters on which the Scottish Parliament can legislate
    a) Civil and Criminal law
    b) Education
    c) Raising of additional taxes
    d) Foreign policy

283. When was the Northern Ireland Parliament first established?
    a) 1922
    b) 1972
    c) 1999
    d) 2001

284. How many members are there in the Northern Ireland Assembly?
    a) 60
    b) 108
    c) 129
    d) 646

285. Decision making powers devolved to Northern Ireland include (Select 3)
    a) Education
    b) The Environment
    c) Defence
    d) Social Services

286. The UK government kept the power to suspend the Northern Ireland Assembly.
    a) Yes. Only if the political leaders no longer agreed to work together or if the Assembly was not working in the interests of the people of Northern Ireland.
    b) No. It can not suspend the Northern Ireland Assembly under any circumstances.

287. How many local authorities are there in London?
    a) 1
    b) 21
    c) 33
    d) 45

288. From where does most of the money for the local authority services come from?
    a) Council tax
    b) VAT
    c) Government
    d) Road tax

289. What percentage of the local authority funding comes from council tax?
    a) 10%
    b) 20%
    c) 30%
    d) 100%

290. What are the mandatory services provided by local authorities? (Give 3 answers)
    a) Education
    b) Social services
    c) Road networks
    d) Planning

291. How often are local elections held?
    a) May every year
    b) Once every 3 years
    c) Once every 5 years
    d) Once every 6 years

292. Many candidates stand for council election as independent candidates and not as members of a political party. Is this statement true or false?
    a) True
    b) False

293. In the UK laws made by Parliament are the highest authority. Is this statement true or false?
    a) True
    b) False

294. If the judges believe that an act of parliament is incompatible with the Human Rights Act, they can change it themselves. Is this statement true or false?
    a) True
    b) False

295. Judges cannot decide whether people are guilty or innocent of serious crimes.
a) True. Only jury will decide whether someone is innocent or guilty.
b) False. They can decide whether someone is innocent or guilty.

296. What must the Government do if the judges agree that the actions of the Government are claimed to be illegal? (select 2 answers)
a) Ignore the judges
b) Change its polices
c) Ask parliament to change the law
d) Overrule the judges

297. What is the name of the largest police force in the United Kingdom?
a) The Metropolitan Police
b) The Surrey Police
c) NYPD
d) The London Police

298. The Government does not have the power to instruct the police to arrest or proceed against an individual. Is this statement true or false?
a) True
b) False

299. Where is the Metropolitan police force based?
a) New Metro Head Office
b) New Scotland Yard
c) Police head office
d) The HQ

300. Who investigate serious complaints against the police? (give 2 answers)
a) The independent Police Complaints Commission
b) The Scotland Yard
c) Parliamentary select committee
d) In Northern Ireland, The police Ombudsman

301. Who controls the finances of the police? (select 2 answers)
a) The government
b) The Scotland Yard
c) Police authorities made up of councillors and magistrates
d) The Queen

302. What are quangos?
   a) Independent organisations and officially called non-departmental public bodies
   b) Semi-independent organisations sponsored by the government; they are officially called non-departmental public bodies

303. Appointments to non-departmental public bodies are usually made by ministers. Is this statement true or false?
   a) True
   b) False

304. Newspapers can publish opinions and run campaigns to influence government.
   a) True. Britain has a free press
   b) False. Newspapers are not allowed to interfere in politics

305. What laws exist regarding political reporting on radio and television? (Give 2 answers)
   a) They have to support the government all of the time
   b) They have to give equal time to rival viewpoints
   c) They should always ignore opposition
   d) Political reporting should be balanced

306. When it comes to political reporting, all newspapers report facts. Is this statement true or false?
   a) True, owners and editors of most newspapers are neutral.
   b) False, owners and editors of most newspapers hold strong political opinions and sometime it is difficult to distinguish fact from opinion

307. In the UK government control the press. Is this statement true or false?
   a) True
   b) False

308. What is the name of the official report of proceedings in Parliament?
   a) The Queen's Speech
   b) The Times
   c) Hansard
   d) Parliament Report

309. When did the United Kingdom become fully democratic?
    a) In 1918 when women gained the right to vote
    b) In 1928 when women were allowed to vote at 21, the same age as men.

310. What is the present voting age?
    a) 16
    b) 18
    c) 21
    d) 24

311. When was the current voting age set?
    a) 1918
    b) 1928
    c) 1969
    d) 1972

312. What rights do all UK-born and naturalised citizen have?
    a) Restricted civic rights
    b) Full civic rights

313. Select 2 of the civic rights all UK-born and naturalised citizen have in the UK
    a) Right to vote
    b) Right to trespass on others property
    c) Right to do jury service
    d) Right to take crown property.

314. You have to be on an electoral register to vote in any elections. Is this statement true or false?
    a) True
    b) False

315. To register to vote you have to fill in a form. Is this statement true or false?
    a) True
    b) False

316. How often is the Electoral register updated?
    a) Every 5 years
    b) Just before every election
    c) Annually
    d) Not very Often

317. When is the Electoral register updated?
   a) September or October each year.
   b) January or February each year.

318. Viewing of the electoral register is supervised. Is this statement true or false?
   a) True
   b) False

319. To have your name placed on the electoral register you have to be 21 or over. True or false?
   a) True
   b) False

320. Where can electoral registers be viewed? (give 2 answers)
   a) Local post offices
   b) Council offices in England and Wales
   c) Libraries
   d) On the internet

321. All permanent residents, who are not British citizens, have the right to vote in all the elections. Is this statement true or false?
   a) True
   b) False

322. Can EU citizens who are resident in the UK vote in National Parliamentary elections?
   a) Yes
   b) No

323. Citizens from which countries are not eligible vote in National Parliamentary elections?
   a) Citizens from Commonwealth
   b) Irish Republic citizens resident in the UK
   c) European citizens
   d) British Citizens

324. In which UK elections can European citizens resident in the UK vote?
   a) All UK elections
   b) All UK elections except National Parliamentary elections
   c) None
   d) Only in National Parliamentary elections

325. In Northern Ireland, once you register yourself on the electoral register it will stay until you make any changes. (true or false)
    a) True
    b) False

326. Citizens from which of the following countries are not eligible to stand for office in the UK?
    a) Citizens from Commonwealth
    b) Irish Republic citizens resident in the UK
    c) European citizens
    d) British Citizens

327. Which of the following groups of people are not allowed to stand for public office? (select more than one answer)
    a) Civil servants
    b) Members of armed forces
    c) Those found guilty of certain criminal offences
    d) Scottish people

328. Under the British system of parliamentary democracy, candidates must be nominated by political parties, to compete for the votes of the electorate in general elections and by-elections. (True or false)
    a) True
    b) False

329. What are the basic requirements for standing for public office? (Give 2 answers)
    a) Must be a citizen of the United Kingdom, Irish Republic, or Commonwealth
    b) Must be a male
    c) Must be over 18 years of age
    d) Must have GCSEs

330. You have to be over 21 to stand for public office. Is this statement true or false?
    a) True
    b) False

331. To become a local councillor, a candidate must have a local connection. Is this statement true or false?
    a) True
    b) False

332. What must a candidate have in order to become a local councillor?
   a) Must be a member of a political party
   b) Candidate must have a local connection with the area, through work, by being on the electoral register, or through renting or owning land or property
   c) Must be a businessman
   d) Must be very well known

333. How do you contact an elected representative? (Give 2 answers)
   a) By going to Parliament and asking for your MP
   b) By looking up a telephone number and calling his or her office
   c) By visiting his/her local office
   d) You cannot do it

334. How can you visit Parliament? (give 2 answers)
   a) Queuing on the day at the public entrance
   b) Getting a ticket to the public galleries from your local MP
   c) You cannot visit parliament unless you are an MP
   d) By buying a ticket online

335. How much do you have to pay to visit Parliament?
   a) A flat fee of £20 to visit both houses of Parliament and many committees
   b) What ever your MP demand for the ticket
   c) General public are not allowed inside Parliament
   d) There is no charge

336. How many member states are there in the Commonwealth?
   a) 175
   b) 100
   c) 53
   d) 26

337. The Commonwealth is a larger international organisation than the United Nations. Is this statement true or false?
   a) True
   b) False

338. Who does the Commonwealth have as its head?
   a) British Prime Minister
   b) The Queen
   c) Prince Philip
   d) The Chancellor

339. Which of the following statements about the Commonwealth is correct?
   a) It is the largest international organisation
   b) It has a membership of 53 states
   c) It represent 50% of the world population
   d) It was established so Britain can rule over them.

340. Almost all of the countries that are members of the Commonwealth are now independent of Britain. Is this statement true or false?
   a) True
   b) False

341. All of the countries in the commonwealth were once part of the British Empire. Is the statement true or false?
   a) True
   b) False

342. Select 2 or more of the countries that are in the commonwealth.
   a) India
   b) United States of America
   c) Malaysia
   d) Canada

343. When did Britain join the European Union?
   a) 1945
   b) 1949
   c) 1957
   d) 1973

344. When was the Treaty of Rome signed?
   a) 25 March 1957
   b) 1 April 1973
   c) 15 June 1949
   d) 2 December 1999

345. How many countries signed the Treaty or Rome?
    a) 4
    b) 6
    c) 10
    d) 15

346. Britain was one of the founding members of European Economic Community. Is this statement true or false?
    a) True
    b) False

347. How many new member countries joined the EU in 2004?
    a) 5
    b) 7
    c) 10
    d) 2

348. How many new member countries joined the EU in 2006?
    a) 2
    b) 5
    c) 10
    d) 12

349. How many member states are there in the European Union at present?
    a) 15
    b) 25
    c) 27
    d) 30

350. The Council of Ministers has no power to propose new laws. Is this statement true or false?
    a) True
    b) False

351. What rights do the citizens of the European Union member states have? (give 2 answers)
    a) Right to travel to any EU country with a valid passport or identity card
    b) Right to work in any EU country (except those that have joined recently)
    c) No right to travel or work in any EU country
    d) The right to work in any country in the world

352. Where does the European Parliament meet?
   a) Milan
   b) Strasbourg and in Brussels
   c) Paris
   d) Geneva

353. In the European Union the Council of Ministers are
   a) Elected during European elections
   b) Government ministers from each member states

354. What powers does the Council of Ministers have in EU?
   a) No Powers
   b) They have powers to propose new laws and decisions regarding the EU

355. The European Parliament scrutinises and debates the proposals, decisions, and expenditure of the European commission. Is this statement true or false?
   a) True
   b) False

356. Where is the European Commission based?
   a) Milan
   b) Strasbourg
   c) Brussels
   d) Geneva

357. European Parliament has the power to refuse to agree European laws proposed by the commission and to check on the spending of the EU funds.
   a) True
   b) False

358. What is the main aim behind the EU today?
   a) It wants the member states to become a single market
   b) To increase member states
   c) Keep out foreign nationals
   d) Become a single country.

359. What is the role of the European Commission? (Give two answers)
    a) Taking care of the day to day running of the organisation
    b) To propose new laws and take important decisions about how the EU is run
    c) Draft proposals for new EU policies and law
    d) Scrutinises and debates the proposals, decisions, and expenditures of the Commission

360. What is the role of the European Parliament?
    a) To scrutinise and debate the proposals, decisions and expenditure of the European Commission
    b) To draft proposals for new EU policies and law
    c) Take care of the day to day running of the organisation
    d) To decide on policy for the EU

361. Why was the European Union first established?
    a) To challenge the UN
    b) On the belief that co-operation between states would reduce the likelihood of another war in Europe
    c) To start Second World War
    d) To counter the threat from Russia

362. When was the Council of Europe established?
    a) 1945
    b) 1949
    c) 1973
    d) 1999

363. Why was the Council of Europe established?
    a) To draw up conventions on human rights, democracy, education, the environment, heath and culture.
    b) Rule the world
    c) Fight the Second World War
    d) To fight the cold war

364. Britain was a founding member of The Council of Europe. (True or false)
    a) True
    b) False

365. European Union law is not legally binding in the UK. Is this statement true or false?
a) True
b) False

366. Which of these statements about EU Directive is correct?
a) EU Directives automatically have force in all EU member states
b) EU Directives must be introduced and observed within EU member states within a specific time frame

367. Most of the countries of Europe are members of the Council of Europe. Is this statement true or false?
a) True
b) False

368. Which international organisation works to prevent war and maintain peace and security?
a) NATO
b) The UN
c) The EU
d) US of A

369. The UK is not a member of United Nations.
a) True
b) False

370. How many countries are there in the UN?
a) 53
b) 100
c) 150
d) Over 190

371. Britain is a permanent Security Council member of the United Nations
a) True
b) False

372. What is the UKs role within the United Nations?
a) UK is one of the permanent member of the UN Security Council
b) UK always has the deciding vote on any issues
c) UK alone makes policy decisions for the UN
d) UK play no role in the UN

373. When was the United Nations set up?
   a) After the First World War
   b) After the Second World War
   c) After the Vietnam war
   d) After the Korean war

374. What are the aims of the UN? (Select more than 1 answer)
   a) To be the ruler of the world
   b) Prevent war
   c) Promote international peace
   d) Promote international security

375. Some of the important agreements produce by the UN include (give 3 answers)
   a) Universal Declaration of Human Rights
   b) Limit the number of hours people can be made to work
   c) Elimination of all forms of Discrimination against women
   d) UN Convention on the Rights of the Child

376. What proportion of the people own their home in the UK?
   a) One-third
   b) Half
   c) Two-thirds
   d) Quarter

377. Two-thirds of people live in rented accommodation in the UK. Is this statement true or false?
   a) True
   b) False

378. People who buy their own home usually pay for it with
   a) Ready cash
   b) Mortgage

379. What is a Mortgage?
   a) A special loan from bank or building society. This loan is paid back with interest , over a long period of time
   b) A special loan from bank or building society. This loan is paid back without interest , over a long period of time

380. If you are having problem paying your mortgage repayment you should
    a) Speak to your bank or building society as soon as you can
    b) Keep quiet and hope things will get better.-

381. In England, if you wish to buy a home, where is the best place to start?
    a) Contact a solicitor
    b) Contact an estate agent
    c) Inform your friends or family
    d) Contact property developer

382. Who do estate agents represent?
    a) Estate agents represent the seller
    b) Estate agents represent the buyer

383. In the UK, except in Scotland, when you find a home you wish to buy you have to make an offer to the seller directly. Is this statement true or false?
    a) True
    b) False

384. Which of these statements is correct about buying a property in UK except in Scotland?
    a) Your first offer must be subject to contract so that you can withdraw if there are reasons why you cannot complete the purchase.
    b) Your first offer is a binding contract and you have to go through with it.

385. Which of these statements is correct about buying a property in Scotland?
    a) The seller sets a price and the buyers make offers over that amount. The agreement become legally binding.
    b) The seller sets a price and the buyers make offers over that amount. The agreement is subject to contract.

386. What is the role of a solicitor in buying a property? (Give 3 answers)
    a) He will carry out number of legal checks on the property
    b) He will carry out checks on the seller
    c) He will deal with the bank to get you a mortgage
    d) He will carry out checks on the local area

387. Who does the bank or building society use when carrying out checks on a property you wish to buy?
a) Local council
b) Surveyor
c) Mortgage broker
d) Bank manager

388. Where is it possible to rent accommodation from? (Give 3 answers)
a) The council
b) Private landlords
c) Banks and building societies
d) Housing associations

389. Most local authorities provide housing. Is this statement true or false?
a) True
b) False

390. Housing provided by the local authorities is often called council housing. Is this statement true or false?
a) True
b) False

391. Can anyone apply for council housing?
a) Yes
b) No

392. How can you apply for council housing?
a) By putting your name down on the council register or list
b) By applying on the internet
c) By approaching the councillors
d) By asking the Mayor

393. Homeless people and families with children get priority when allocating council housing. Is this statement true or false?
a) True
b) False

394. In many areas of the UK there is a shortage of council accommodation. Is this statement true or false?
a) True
b) False

395. Which of these statements is true about council housing?
    a) Council accommodations are allocated on first come first serve basis.
    b) Homeless people and families with children get priority when allocating council housing.

396. What is meant by housing associations?
    a) They are formed by house owners in a neighbourhood to protect their area
    b) They are independent not for profit organisations which provide housing for rent.

397. How can housing associations help people buy their own property.
    a) By selling the properties they own cheaply
    b) By means of shared ownership, which help people buy part of a house or flat if they cannot afford to buy all of it at once.

398. What is a tenancy agreement?
    a) A document explaining the conditions or rules you must follow while renting a property
    b) A receipt given by your landlord for the rent you pay.

399. Which of these statements is correct about tenancy agreement?
    a) You don't need to sign that document
    b) The agreement also contains a list of inventory in the property.

400. Why will you be asked to pay a deposit when you rent a property?
    a) To keep the landlord happy.
    b) To cover the cost of any damage.

401. The landlord can keep the deposit paid by the tenant at the end of the tenancy. Is this statement true or false?
    a) True
    b) False

402. Which of these statements is true about deposit you pay when renting a property?
    a) It is usually equal to one months rent.
    b) It is usually equal to one years rent.

403. Which of these statements is true about rent?
   a) The landlord can raise the rent in the middle of your tenancy without your agreement.
   b) The landlord cannot raise the rent in the middle of your tenancy without your agreement

404. What happens if you want to end your tenancy before the fixed time?
   a) You do not have to pay the rent for the agreed full period of your tenancy
   b) You usually have to pay the rent for the agreed full period of your tenancy

405. The landlord can use threats or violence to force a tenant to leave, since he own the property. Is this statement true or false?
   a) True
   b) False

406. Which of these statements is true?
   a) It is not a criminal offence for a landlord to force a tenant to leave without an order from court.
   b) It is a criminal offence for a landlord to force a tenant to leave without an order from court.

407. Is it unlawful for a landlord to discriminate against someone looking for accommodation because they are disabled?
   a) Yes
   b) No

408. In order to get council accommodation you need to prove (Give 3 answers)
   a) You have priority need.
   b) You have a connection with the area.
   c) You have enough money to pay the rent
   d) You have not made yourself intentionally homeless.

409. Who can you ask for help if you find yourself homeless? (Give 3 answers)
   a) The housing department of the local authority.
   b) Department of Housing
   c) The citizens Advice Bureau.
   d) A charity called Shelter

410. What options do you have when paying the water rates? (Give 2 answers)
   a) You can pay it in one payment
   b) You can ask the council to pay it
   c) You can pay it in instalment
   d) You don't have to pay if you are renting the property.

411. The cost of the water usually depends on the size of your property if you do not have a water meter. Is this statement true or false?
   a) True
   b) False

412. In Northern Ireland water rates are currently included in the council tax. Is this statement true or false?
   a) True
   b) False

413. In the UK (except Northern Ireland) water rates are included in the council tax. Is this statement true or false?
   a) True
   b) False

414. All properties in the UK have electricity supplied at
   a) 110 volts
   b) 240 volts

415. Where can you find the Emergency numbers for your gas, water or electricity suppliers?
   a) On the bill
   b) Yellow pages
   c) Phone book
   d) Local newspapers

416. How can you find out which company supplies your electricity?
   a) By calling the local police station
   b) By Calling Energywatch

417. Which company do you need to call to find out who supplies your gas?
   a) BT
   b) Transco

418. What two numbers can you dial for emergency calls for police, fire or ambulance service?
   a) 999
   b) 100
   c) 112
   d) 911

419. Where can you get advice about prices or about changing your phone company?
   a) Local council
   b) Ofcom

420. What methods of payment can you use to make calls from public payphones? (Select 3 answers)
   a) Cash
   b) Pre-paid phone cards
   c) SIM cards
   d) Credit or debit cards

421. If you get your gas, water or electricity supply cut off for non payment of bill, you can get them reconnected free of charge once the payment is made. Is this statement true or false?
   a) True
   b) False

422. Where can you find information on how to pay for water, gas, electricity and the telephone?
   a) By asking your friend.
   b) It can be found on the back of each bill.

423. It is possible to pay your bills by standing order or direct debit. Is this statement true or false?
   a) True
   b) False

424. Most utility companies offer budget scheme which allow you to pay a fixed sum every month. Is this statement true or false?
   a) True
   b) False

425. Who collects the household waste?
 a) Private firms
 b) Local authority

426. How often is household waste collected at present?
 a) Once a month
 b) Twice a month
 c) Once a week
 d) Twice a week

427. How can you throw away large items like a bed, wardrobe or a fridge?
 a) Leave it with your household waste.
 b) Leave it by the side of a road.
 c) Contact the local authority to arrange collection.
 d) Burn it in the back garden

428. Which of these statements is true about disposing of waste?
 a) You can leave your business waste with your household waste.
 b) It is a criminal offence to dump rubbish anywhere.

429. How can you recycle your rubbish?
 a) If your council collects recyclable waste keep it separate
 b) You can take it to recycling centres
 c) Mix it with your normal waste hoping they all get recycled.
 d) You cannot do that at present as we don't have any facilities

430. What options do you have when paying the council tax? (Select 3 answers)
 a) You can pay it in one payment
 b) You can pay it in two instalments
 c) You can pay it over 2 year period
 d) You can pay it in 10 instalments

431. You do not have to register to pay Council Tax if you are a tenant of the property. Is this statement true or false?
 a) True
 b) False

432. You must register to pay Council Tax when you move into a new property, either as the owner or the tenant. Is this statement true or false?
 a) True
 b) False

433. The amount of Council Tax you pay depends on the (give 2 answers)
   a) Size of your property
   b) The household income
   c) Value of your property
   d) Age of your property

434. What reduction can you get on your Council tax if only one person live a property?
   a) 10%
   b) 20%
   c) 25%
   d) 50%

435. When can you get Council Tax Benefit? (give 3 answers)
   a) If you are on a low income
   b) If you are on Income Support
   c) If you are on Jobseekers Allowance
   d) If you are a foreign national

436. If you have problem with your neighbours, they can usually be solved by threatening them. Is this statement true or false?
   a) True
   b) False

437. If you cannot solve the problem with your neighbour by speaking to them, you can (Give 2 answers)
   a) Tell your friends
   b) Speak to the local authority
   c) Speak to the landlord if you are a tenant.
   d) Speak to your bank or building society

438. Neighbours who cause a very serious nuisance may be taken to court and can be evicted from their home. Is this statement true or false?
   a) True
   b) False

439. What are the things to do if you have a problem neighbour? (Select 2)
   a) Keep a record of exact problems with that neighbour
   b) Keep a record of when they started
   c) Always be ready to confront him/her
   d) Call the police every time you have a problem

440. Bank notes in the UK come in denominations of £5, £10, £20, £50. True or false?
a) True
b) False

441. Bank notes printed by Northern Ireland and Scotland are not valid anywhere else. Is this statement true or false?
a) True
b) False

442. How many countries in the European Union have adopted the Euro as their common currency in 2002?
a) 10
b) 12
c) 15
d) 25

443. The UK government will adopt the Euro if the British Parliament votes for it. Is this statement true or false?
a) True
b) False

444. Where can you get or change foreign currency? (Select 3 answers)
a) At bank or building societies
b) Supermarkets
c) Large post offices
d) Exchange shops or bureaux de change

445. What kind of IDs do you require to open a bank or building society account? (Give 2 answers)
a) Documents to prove your identity like passport or driving licence
b) Travel card
c) Something with your address on it like household bills
d) Letter from your landlord

446. What are cash cards?
a) They allow you to pay for goods and services
b) They allow you to use cash machines to withdraw money from your account.

447. What is a debit card?
   a) It allows you to borrow money from your bank.
   b) It allows you to pay for things without using cash.

448. Credit and store cards do not draw money from your bank account. Is this statement true or false?
   a) True
   b) False

449. If you were refused a loan, you have the right to ask the reason why. Is this statement true or false?
   a) True
   b) False

450. What kind of information do the banks need to make a decision about a loan?
   a) Your occupation
   b) Salary
   c) Previous credit record
   d) All of the above

451. Which of these statements about credit unions are true?
   a) Interest rates in credit unions are usually higher than banks and building societies.
   b) Credit unions are financial co-operatives owned and controlled by their members.

452. Insurance is compulsory if you have a car or motorcycle. Is this statement true or false?
   a) True
   b) False

453. Why do people buy insurance when they travel abroad? (Give 2 answers)
   a) In case they lose their luggage
   b) They get discount when they buy it from the travel agent
   c) In case they need medical treatment.
   d) Because they were told to

454. Who can claim social security benefits?
   a) Sick and disabled
   b) Unemployed
   c) Those on low income
   d) All of the above

455. People who do not have legal rights of residence in the UK can usually receive benefits. Is this statement true or false?
   a) True
   b) False

456. What does NHS stand for?
   a) National Heath System
   b) National Health Service
   c) Nations Health service
   d) New Health Service

457. When did NHS begin?
   a) 1938
   b) 1948
   c) 1958
   d) 1968

458. Which of these statements about the NHS is true?
   a) It provides unemployed with free healthcare and treatment
   b) It provide all residents with free healthcare and treatment

459. What does GP stand for?
   a) Good practitioners
   b) General Practitioners

460. If you need to see a specialist in a hospital, what do you have to do?
   a) You must book an appointment with that specialist
   b) You must go to your GP first.

461. When can you attend a hospital without a GP's Letter?
   a) Only when your GP is on holiday
   b) Only if you have an emergency

462. What must you do if you do not have a medical card?
    a) Ask the GP's receptionist for one
    b) Ask the GP's receptionist for a form to send to the local health authority

463. Why may some GPs refuse to accept you?
    a) Sometimes GPs have many patients and are unable to accept new ones.
    b) Some GPs may not take on foreign nationals.

464. Which of these statements about GP consultations is true?
    a) Everything you tell the GP is not completely confidential and can be passed on to anyone else without your permission.
    b) Everything you tell the GP is completely confidential and cannot be passed on to anyone else without your permission.

465. Sometime you might have to wait several days before you can see a doctor. Is this statement true or false?
    a) True
    b) False

466. Is it possible to make an urgent appointment to see your GP?
    a) Yes. If you need immediate medical attention.
    b) No. You have to wait.

467. Do GPs visit patients at home?
    a) Yes. Only in exceptional circumstances
    b) No. They do not have time.

468. Who are eligible for free prescription? (select more than one answers)
    a) Under 16s
    b) Over 50s
    c) Mothers who are pregnant or with babies less than 12 months old.
    d) Under 19 and in full-time education

469. Treatment from the GP is very costly. Is this statement true or false?
    a) True
    b) False

470. How can you make an appointment to see the GP?
    a) By writing a letter.
    b) By Phone
    c) By visiting the surgery
    d) By sending a fax

471. What can you do if you or your child feels unwell and you need infor-mation or advice? (select 3 answers)
    a) Ask your pharmacist
    b) Talk to your friends
    c) Speak to a nurse by phoning NHS Direct
    d) Use NHS direct website

472. What can you do if you or child feel unwell and you need to see a doctor or nurse? (select 2 answers)
    a) Visit an NHS walk in centre
    b) Make and appointment to see your GP or a nurse working in the surgery.
    c) Phone the hospital
    d) Dial 999

473. What can you do if you or your child feel unwell and need urgent medi-cal treatment? (select 2 answers)
    a) Contact your local hospital
    b) Contact your GP
    c) Call 999 for an ambulance
    d) Go to your pharmacy

474. Where can you take your prescription to get the medicine you need?(select 2 answers)
    a) To your GP
    b) To the nearest hospital
    c) To a pharmacy
    d) To a supermarket where they have a pharmacy

475. What does NHS walk in centres offer?
    a) They provide treatment for private patients.
    b) They provide treatment for minor injuries and illnesses seven days a week

476. What is NHS Direct Online?
  a) Is a website providing online treatment for illnesses
  b) Is a website providing information about heath services and several medical conditions and treatments.

477. If you are an in-patient in a hospital
  a) You will receive all you meals free of charge
  b) You have to pay for all your meals

478. You will attend the outpatients department
  a) If you need a minor test at a hospital
  b) If you need to stay overnight at a hospital.

479. Most people don't pay for their dental treatment. Is this statement true or false?
  a) True
  b) False

480. NHS dentists charge more than private dentists. Is this statement true or false?
  a) True
  b) False

481. Who is eligible for free dental treatment? (select 3 answers)
  a) People under 18 (except in Wales)
  b) Pregnant women and women with babies under 12 months old
  c) People over 45
  d) People on income support, Jobseekers' allowance or Pension Credit Guarantee.

482. Who is eligible for free eye tests and glasses? (select 3 answers)
  a) Children
  b) People over 60
  c) People receiving certain benefits
  d) Students between the ages 18-25

483. Where can you receive anti-natal care? (select more than 1 answer)
  a) Local hospitals
  b) Local health centres
  c) Local pharmacists
  d) Special antenatal clinics

484. Some GPs do not provide maternity services. Is this statement true or false?
   a) True
   b) False

485. Midwives works in hospitals or health centres. (true or false)
   a) True
   b) False

486. Which of these statements is true about child birth?
   a) It is not common for the father to attend the birth
   b) In the UK women usually have their babies in hospital

487. Who is a health visitor?
   a) She or he is a qualified nurse
   b) She or he is a doctor

488. Health visitors can advise you about caring for your baby. Is this statement true or false?
   a) True
   b) False

489. Where can you get information on maternity and anti-natal services in your area? (give 3 answers)
   a) Local health authority
   b) Health visitor
   c) Your pharmacist
   d) Your GP

490. You must register your baby with the Register Office within six months. Is this statement true or false?
   a) True
   b) False

491. If the parents are not married but want both names on the child's birth certificate, what do they have to do?
   a) Only the mother can register the birth if they are not married.
   b) Both mother and father must be present when they register their baby.

492. Education in the UK is free but not compulsory for children between the ages of 5 and 16 (4-16 in Northern Ireland)
   a) True
   b) False

493. The parent or guardian may be prosecuted if their child does not go to school, arrive on time or attend for the whole school year. Is this statement true or false?
   a) True
   b) False

494. In England and Wales Primary school is attended by children of ages
   a) 5 to 11
   b) 4 to 11
   c) 5 to 12
   d) 4 to 12

495. What can children do once they finish secondary school at the age of 16? (select more than 1 answer)
   a) They can leave school
   b) They can continue with their education until they are 17 or 18
   c) They can apply for university

496. At what age do children attend secondary school in England, Wales and N.Ireland?
   a) 11
   b) 9
   c) 7
   d) 4

497. Where can you find information on schools in your area
   a) From your local education authority
   b) From the Yellow pages

498. Why do some parents apply for several secondary schools when they need a place for their child?
   a) Because in some areas, getting a secondary school place in a preferred school can be difficult.
   b) Because they cannot make their mind up as to where to send their children.

499. In the UK parents have to pay for education, school uniform and sports ware. Is this statement true or false?
a) True
b) False

500. Which of these statements are true about faith schools?
a) They are independent schools
b) They are linked to certain faith or religion

501. What is meant by integrated schools?
a) In Northern Ireland they aim to integrate boys and girls
b) In Northern Ireland they aim to bring children of different religions together.

502. What are independent schools?
a) They are private schools
b) They are run by local education authorities

503. Independent secondary schools are sometimes called
a) Community schools
b) Public schools

504. What percentage of children in the UK attends private schools?
a) 5%
b) 8%
c) 10%
d) 12%

505. In independent schools parents must pay the full cost of their child's education. (True or false?)
a) True
b) False

506. All state, primary and secondary schools in England, Wales and Northern Ireland follow the National Curriculum. Is this statement true or false?
a) True
b) False

507. Select some of the subjects covered by National Curriculum (Select 3)
a) Art and Design
b) English
c) Home science
d) Citizenship

508. By law, schools must provide religious education but parents are allowed to withdraw their children from theses lessons. Is this statement true or false?
   a) True
   b) False

509. In England children take Key Stage tests (called SATs) when they are
   a) 7,9 and 11 years old
   b) 7,11 and 14 years old
   c) 7,11 and 16 years old
   d) 9,14 and 16 years old

510. In Wales teachers assess and report on their pupil's progress and achievements at 7 and 11. Is this statement true or false?
   a) True
   b) False

511. In Scotland teachers test individual children between the ages of 5 to 14 rather than as a group. Is this statement true or false?
   a) True
   b) False

512. Where can children get careers advice when they are 14?
   a) From citizen advice bureau
   b) From Connexions

513. What are the roles of the school governing body? (Select 3)
   a) Decides on how the schools is run
   b) Decides on how the schools administered
   c) Decides who can attend school
   d) Produces reports on the progress of the school.

514. Can parents serve in the school governing body?
   a) Yes
   b) No

515. How many days must schools be open a year?
   a) 190
   b) 210
   c) 250
   d) 300

516. Young people from families of low income can get financial help with their studies when they leave school at 16. This is called
   a) Unemployment Benefit (UB)
   b) Education Maintenance Allowance (EMA)

517. Which of the courses listed below can be considered as skills for Life courses? (Give 2 answers)
   a) Literacy courses
   b) Interior design courses
   c) Numeracy courses
   d) Water colour painting courses

518. Where can you get information of adult education classes? (Select 2)
   a) Local libraries
   b) National Newspapers
   c) College or adult education centres
   d) Yellow pages

519. Less young people go to university now than in the past. Is this statement true or false?
   a) True
   b) False

520. Most students in England, Wales and Northern Ireland have to pay towards the cost of their tuition fees. Is this statement true or false?
   a) True
   b) False

521. At present how much can universities charge up to, for a year, for their tuition fees?
   a) £2000
   b) £3000
   c) £4000
   d) £5000

522. In Scotland there are no tuitions fee for universities, but students have to pay back some of the cost of their education in payment called endowment. Is this statement true or false?
   a) True
   b) False

523. In the UK (except in Scotland) university students do not have to pay anything towards their fees before or during their studies. Is this statement true or false?
    a) True
    b) False

524. Is there any help available for low income families towards university tuition fees
    a) Yes. Some families can receive grants.
    b) No. They can only take out low interest loans

525. In the UK (except in Scotland) the university students do not have to pay anything towards their fees before or during their studies.
    a) True. The government pays their tuition fees and then charges for them when a student start working after university
    b) False. You have to pay before you start university.

526. In the UK Many museums and galleries are free. Is this statement true or false?
    a) True
    b) False

527. Where can you find information about theatre, cinema, music and exhibitions? (Select more than one answer)
    a) Local news papers
    b) Local libraries
    c) Yellow pages
    d) Tourist information offices

528. If a child is below the age of the classification of a film, they should not watch it in the cinema but they can watch the DVD. Is this statement true or false?
    a) True
    b) False

529. What does the film classification R18 mean?
    a) No one under 18 is allowed to see or rent the film
    b) No one over18 is allowed to see or rent the film
    c) No one under 18 is allowed see or rent the film, which is only available in specially licensed cinema
    d) Children under 15 are not allowed to see or rent the film

530. What does the film classification U mean?
   a) Suitable for anyone aged 4 years and over
   b) Suitable for everyone but some parts of the film might be unsuitable for children. Their parents should decide
   c) Suitable for anyone aged 12 years and over
   d) Suitable for anyone aged 8 years and over

531. What does the film classification PG mean?
   a) Suitable for anyone aged 4 years and over
   b) Suitable for everyone but some parts of the film might be unsuitable for children. Their parents should decide
   c) Suitable for anyone aged 12 years and over
   d) Suitable for anyone aged 8 years and over

532. Film classification 12 or 12a means children are not allowed to see or rent the film unless they are with an adult. Is this statement true or false?
   a) True
   b) False

533. Who should have a valid television licence?
   a) Only the people with colour TV should have a valid TV licence
   b) Anyone with any device which is used for watching or recording TV programmes should have a valid TV licence

534. One licence covers all of the equipment at one address. Is this statement true or false?
   a) True
   b) False

535. If different people rent different rooms in a shared house only one of them need to buy a TV licence. Is this statement true or false?
   a) True
   b) False

536. How long does a TV licence last?
   a) 6 months
   b) 1 year
   c) 18 months
   d) 2 years

537. What can happen if you watch television not covered by a TV licence?
a) You will be told off.
b) You risk prosecution and a fine.

538. Where can you buy a TV licence? (Select 3 answers)
a) Online
b) Pay Point outlets
c) Post offices
d) Supermarkets

539. How much does the current colour TV licence cost?
a) 151.50
b) 131.50

540. Who are eligible for discount on TV licence fee?
a) People who are blind
b) People aged 75 or over
c) Unemployed people
d) People who only watch satellite television

541. What is the National Trust?
a) It's a type of building society
b) It's a charity that works to preserve important buildings and countryside in the UK

542. To drink alcohol in a pub you must be 16 years or over. Is this statement true or false?
a) True
b) False

543. What is the minimum age for buying alcohol in a supermarket or in an off-licence?
a) 16
b) 18
c) 19
d) 21

544. What is the minimum age for buying a lottery ticket?
a) 15
b) 16
c) 18
d) 21

545. At what age are people allowed into betting shop and gambling clubs?
a) When they are 16 and over
b) When they are 18 and over
c) When they are 21 and over
d) When they are 24 and over

546. All dogs in public places must wear a collar showing the name and address of the owner. Is this statement true or false?
a) True
b) False

547. Travelling on public transport in the rush hour is always cheaper. Is this statement true or false?
a) True
b) False

548. Who are eligible for discounted tickets on public transport? (select more than one answer)
a) People aged 60 or over
b) Disabled people
c) People working full time
d) Students and people under 26

549. Taxis and cabs with no licence plate are always cheap but safer to travel. Is this statement true or false?
a) True
b) False

550. At what age can you drive a car or motorcycle?
a) 15
b) 16
c) 17
d) 18

551. What are the three stages to get a driving licence?
a) Buy a second hand car
b) Apply for a provisional licence
c) Pass a written test
d) Pass a practical driving test

552. When a learner driver drive a car he should have someone who (select 2)
   a) Is your friend
   b) Is 21 years or over
   c) Should own that car
   d) Has had a full licence for over three years

553. You need a full licence while you are learning to drive. Is this statement true or false?
   a) True
   b) False

554. If you have a licence from a country outside the EU, how long can you use it to drive in the UK?
   a) 6 months
   b) 12 months
   c) 18 months
   d) Until your licence is valid

555. If you have a licence from a country outside the EU, what do you have to do after 12 months?
   a) Must get a provisional licence and pass the UK practical driving test
   b) Must get a provisional licence and pass both the UK theory and practical driving test

556. Is it a criminal offence to have a car without a proper motor insurance?
   a) Yes
   b) No

557. It is illegal to allow someone to use your car if they are not insured to drive it. Is this statement true or false?
   a) True
   b) False

558. You do not need an MOT certificate if you car is more than 3 years old. Is this statement true or false?
   a) True
   b) False

559. Which of the following do you need in order to have your vehicle legally on the road? (select 3 answers)
   a) Road tax
   b) Valid MOT
   c) Less than 3 year old vehicle
   d) Valid insurance for your vehicle

560. Where can you get an MOT certificate for your car?
   a) From the Ministry of transport
   b) From and approved garage

561. Everyone in a vehicle except the people in the back seat must wear a seat belt. Is this statement true or false?
   a) True
   b) False

562. What is the speed limit for cars and motorcycles in a built-up area? (unless a sign shows otherwise)
   a) 15 miles per hour
   b) 30 miles per hour
   c) 60 miles per hour
   d) 70 miles per hour

563. What is the speed limit for cars and motorcycles on motorways and dual carriageways? (unless a sign shows otherwise)
   a) 30 miles per hour
   b) 40 miles per hour
   c) 60 miles per hour
   d) 70 miles per hour

564. Is it an arrestable offence to drive a car while over the limit or refuse to give a breathalyser test?
   a) Yes
   b) No

565. What is the penalty for people who drink and drive?
   a) Severe warning from the police
   b) Disqualification from driving for a long period of time

566. If you are involved in a road accident which of the following must you not do? (select 2 answers)
    a) Drive away without stopping
    b) Give your details to the other drivers
    c) Get the details from the other drivers
    d) Admit fault

567. What do you do if you are involved in a road accident?
    a) Give your details to other drivers and to the police
    b) Get the names, addresses, vehicle registration numbers and the insurance details of the other drivers.
    c) Make note of everything that happened and contact your insurance company as soon as possible.
    d) All of the above

568. Not everyone in the UK is allowed to work. Is this statement true?
    a) Yes. Some people need work permits.
    b) No. Anyone in the UK can work.

569. How can you find out about job vacancies?
    a) In local and national newspapers
    b) Jobcentre
    c) Employment agencies
    d) All of the above

570. Jobcentre plus is run by
    a) The Home office
    b) The department for work and pension
    c) Ministry of Employment
    d) Local authorities

571. What kind of service can you get from jobcentre plus? (Select more than 1 answer)
    a) Help and advice on finding a job
    b) Help and advice on applying for jobs
    c) Help and advice on finding accommodation
    d) Help and advice on claiming benefits

572. If you have qualifications from another country , you can find out how they compare with qualifications in the UK
   a) At the jobcentre plus
   b) At the National Academic Recognition information centre

573. For many jobs you need to fill in an application form or send a copy of your CV. Is this statement true or false?
   a) True
   b) False

574. What does CV stand for?
   a) Cover letter
   b) Curriculum vitae

575. What is the benefit of writing a covering letter with an application form? (Give 2 answers)
   a) You can give more detailed information on why you are applying for the job.
   b) People like to read letters than looking at the application form.
   c) You can give more detailed information on why you think you are suitable.
   d) Employers can check your hand writing.

576. It is important to type any letters and your CV on a computer or word processor. Is this statement true or false?
   a) True
   b) False

577. Why is it important to be honest about your qualifications and experience in an interview?
   a) If an employer later finds out that you gave incorrect information, you might have to pay the employer compensation
   b) If an employer later finds out that you gave incorrect information, you might lose your job.

578. Can you ask any questions to the employer at an interview?
   a) Yes. It shows you are interested.
   b) No. It's rude to ask questions.

579. For what kind of work you be checked, for a criminal record? (Give 2 answers)
   a) If your work involve working with customers
   b) If your work involve working with children
   c) If your work involve working with vulnerable people.
   d) If your work involve working in a factory.

580. Where can you get more information about criminal record check?
   a) From the local library.
   b) From the Home Office Criminal Records Bureau.

581. Where can you find information on courses which can help you train?
   a) Local library
   b) Local colleges
   c) Certain website (www.worktrain.gov.uk)
   d) All of the above

582. What are the benefits of doing voluntary work? (Select 2 answers)
   a) It's a good way to support your local community and organisations which depends on volunteers.
   b) You can get yourself fit.
   c) It provides useful experience that can help with future applications.
   d) It will stop you getting bored.

583. It is illegal to discriminate against a person because of their religion. Is this statement true or false?
   a) True
   b) False

584. It is illegal to discriminate against a person because of their sexual orientation. Is this statement true or false?
   a) True
   b) False

585. It is illegal to discriminate against a person because of their age. Is this statement true or false?
   a) True
   b) False

586. It is illegal to discriminate against a person because of their sex. Is this statement true or false?
   a) True
   b) False

587. It is illegal to discriminate against a person because of their nationality, race, colour or ethnic group. Is this statement true or false?
   a) True
   b) False

588. From the list below, which are examples of discrimination against some-one at work because of their sex, colour, disability, religion or age?
   a) Refusal of work
   b) Refusal of training or promotion
   c) If they were treated less favourably
   d) All of the above

589. The law state that men and women who do the same job, or work of equal value, should receive equal pay. Is the statement true or false?
   a) True
   b) False

590. In Northern Ireland, the law also bans discrimination on the grounds of religious belief or political opinion. Is this statement true or false?
   a) True
   b) False

591. Discrimination law does not apply when it involves working for someone in their own home. Is this statement true or false?
   a) True
   b) False

592. Where can you get more information on law and racial discrimination?
   a) The Law society
   b) The Commission for Racial Equality

593. Which organisation can help with sex discrimination issues?
   a) The Equal Opportunities Commission
   b) The Disability Rights Commission

594. Which organisation can help with disability issues?
    a) The Equal Opportunities Commission
    b) The Disability Rights Commission

595. Can men and women be victims of sexual harassment at work?
    a) Yes
    b) No. Only women.

596. Which of the following could be considered a form of sexual harassment? (Select 3 answers)
    a) Comments about the way you look that makes you feel uncomfortable
    b) Indecent remarks
    c) Talking about football
    d) Comments or questions about your sex life.

597. What is the first thing to when sexual harassment happens to you at work?
    a) Ignore it at first
    b) Tell your friends, colleague or trade union representative and ask the person to stop.

598. Who can you ask for help if your employer does not deal with sexual harassment to your satisfaction?
    a) The Equal Opportunities Commission
    b) Your trade union
    c) Citizens Advice Bureau
    d) Very difficult to get help on this issue.

599. What should the contract of employment include?
    a) Your responsibilities, pay, working hours, holidays, sick pay and pension
    b) Only the employers name and address.

600. When should you receive the contract of employment once you start work?
    a) Within 1 month
    b) Within 2 months
    c) Within 3 months
    d) Within 6 months

601. From October 2006, the minimum wage for workers aged 22 and above is
    a) £6.05 an hour
    b) £5.35 an hour
    c) £4.45 an hour
    d) £3.30 an hour

602. From October 2006, the minimum wage for workers aged 18 - 21 is
    a) £6.05 an hour
    b) £5.35 an hour
    c) £4.45 an hour
    d) £3.30 an hour

603. From October 2006, the minimum wage for workers aged 16 - 17 is
    a) £6.05 an hour
    b) £5.35 an hour
    c) £4.45 an hour
    d) £3.30 an hour

604. Your employer cannot require you to work more hours than the hours agreed on your contract. Is this statement true or false?
    a) True
    b) False

605. Which government department is responsible for collecting taxes
    a) Central Bank
    b) HM Revenue and Customs

606. How is the money collected from taxes spent?
    a) For services such as roads, education, police and armed forces.
    b) Building accommodation by property developers

607. Almost everyone in the UK, who is in paid work, including self-employed people, must pay National Insurance contributions. Is this statement true or false?
    a) True
    b) False

608. How is the money raised by National Insurance contributions spent?
    a) On defence
    b) Fund the State Retirement Pension
    c) Fund the National Health Service.
    d) On Education

609. How do people pay their National Insurance contributions? (Select 2 answers)
a) Employees will have their NI contributions deducted from their pay by their employer every week or month.
b) People who are self-employed will pay NI contributions themselves.
c) Everyone pays their NI contributions at the end of the year.
d) It is taken out of everyone's bank by direct debit every month.

610. Anyone who does not pay enough NI contributions will not be able to receive certain benefits such as (Select more than 1 answer)
a) Housing benefit
b) Jobseekers allowance
c) Maternity Pay
d) Full state retirement pension.

611. Which of these statements about NI contributions by self-employed people is correct?
a) Class 2 contributions are paid every year.
b) Class 4 contributions are paid alongside their income tax.

612. How often are class 2 NI contributions by self-employed people paid?
a) Every month
b) Every three months
c) Every 6 months
d) Every 12 months

613. At what age are all young people in the UK sent a National Insurance Number?
a) 15
b) 16
c) 17
d) 18

614. How can you apply for a National Insurance Number? (Select 2)
a) Through Jobcentre Plus
b) Through local Social Security Office
c) Through Post Office
d) Through Home Office

615. What kinds of documents are usually needed when applying for an NI number? (Select 3)
   a) Passport
   b) Birth certificate
   c) Home Office document allowing you to stay in the country
   d) A reference letter from your solicitor

616. Where can you get information about registering for a National Insurance number?
   a) Employment helpline.
   b) National Insurance Registration Helpline.

617. Which of theses statements about the state pension is correct?
   a) Everyone in the UK will get a State Pension when they retire
   b) Everyone in the UK who has paid enough NI contributions will get a State Pension when they retire

618. Where can you get free advice on occupational and personal Pensions?
   a) The Social Security helpline
   b) The Pension Advisory Service

619. You can get advice about your personal pensions from Independent Financial Advisers. Is this statement True or false?
   a) True
   b) False

620. You normally have to pay for services provided by Independent Financial Advisors. Is this statement true or false?
   a) True
   b) False

621. What is the current state pension age for men?
   a) 60
   b) 65
   c) 70
   d) 75

622. What is the current state pension age for women?
   a) 60
   b) 65
   c) 70
   d) 75

623. When will the women's state pension age increase to 65?
   a) In stages between 2010 and 2020
   b) In stages between 2008 and 2015

624. Employers have a legal duty to make sure the workplace is safe. Is this statement true or false?
   a) True
   b) False

625. Employees have a legal duty to follow safety regulations and to work safely and responsibly. Is this statement true or false?
   a) True
   b) False

626. You shouldn't raise any issues about health and safety, because doing so may lead to your dismissal. Is this statement true or false?
   a) True
   b) False

627. Who can you talk to if you are worried about health and safety at your workplace? (Select more than one answer)
   a) Your supervisor
   b) Your employer
   c) Your trade union representative
   d) Your family and friends

628. What are trade unions?
   a) They are organisations that aim to improve the pay and working conditions of their members.
   b) They are organisations that aim to get wealthy by charging subscription from its members.

629. Can an employer dismiss you for belonging to a trade union?
   a) Yes
   b) No

630. Can you choose whether to join a trade union or not?
   a) Yes
   b) No

631. Where can you find details of trade unions in the UK?
    a) Department of Trade and Industry website
    b) Trades Union Congress (TUC) website

632. You can choose whether to join a trade union or not and your employer cannot dismiss you or treat you unfairly for being a union member. Is this statement true or false?
    a) True
    b) False

633. Who should you speak to, if you have problems of any kind at work? (Select 3 answers)
    a) Your friends and family
    b) Your supervisor
    c) Your manager
    d) Your trade union representative

634. ACAS stand for Advisory, Conciliation and Arbitration Service. Is this statement true or false?
    a) True
    b) False

635. If you have any kind of problem at work, you can get advice from the Citizen Advice Bureau. Is this statement true or false?
    a) True
    b) False

636. An employee can be dismissed immediately for serious misconduct at work. Is this statement true or false?
    a) True
    b) False

637. Anyone who cannot do their job properly, or is unacceptably late or absent from work, should be
    a) Dismissed immediately
    b) Given a warning

638. An employee will be given a warning if they are; (Select 3)
    a) Unacceptably late.
    b) Absent from work for long periods of time without a valid reason.
    c) Earn too much.
    d) Cannot do their job properly.

639. If an employee's work, punctuality or attendance doest not improve even after a warning, the employer can give him
a) Another warning
b) Notice to leave his job

640. It is against the law for employers to dismiss someone from work unfairly. Is this statement true or false?
a) True
b) False

641. Can you get compensation if you were dismissed from work unfairly or life at work was made so difficult that you felt you had to leave?
a) Yes
b) No

642. What is an Employment Tribunal?
a) It is a court which specialises in employment matters.
b) It is an employment agency

643. Where can you take your employer to if you think you were dismissed unfairly?
a) To a small claims court
b) To an Employment Tribunal

644. If you are dismissed from your job, it is important to get advice on your case
a) Within 12 months of your dismissal
b) As soon as possible

645. Who can advice you on unfair dismissal?
a) your trade union representative
b) A solicitor or a Law Centre
c) Citizen's Advice Bureau
d) All of the above

646. When will you be entitled for redundancy pay? (select 2)
a) If you lose your job because the company you work for no longer needs someone to do your job.
b) If you lose your job because you cannot do the job properly.
c) If you lose your job because you hand in your notice.
d) If you lose your job because the company you worked for cannot afford to employ you.

647. The amount of money you may receive as redundancy depends on the amount of money you have earned as wages. Is this statement true or false?
a) True
b) False

648. The amount of money you may receive as redundancy depends on the length of time you have been employed. Is this statement true or false?
a) True
b) False

649. Only some people who become unemployed can claim Jobseeker's Allowance. Is this statement true or false?
a) True
b) False

650. To what age group is Jobseeker's Allowance available? (Select 2 answers)
a) For men 18-60
b) For men 18-65
c) For women 18-65
d) For women 18-60

651. Unemployed 16 and 17 year olds may be able to claim Young Person's Bridging Allowance. Is this statement true or false?
a) True
b) False

652. Where do you need to apply for Jobseekers Allowance and Young Person's Bridging Allowance if you are unemployed?
a) Local authority
b) Jobcentre plus

653. What is the New Deal?
a) It is a government programme that aims to give unemployed people the help and support they need to get into work.
b) It is a government program to get people to change jobs.

654. Young people who have been unemployed for 18 months are usually required to join the New Deal if they wish to continue receiving benefit. Is this statement true or false?
a) True
b) False

655. Adults who have been unemployed for 18 months are usually required to join the New Deal if they wish to continue receiving benefit. Is this statement true or false?
    a) True
    b) False

656. How often should self-employed people send their business accounts to HM Revenue and Customs?
    a) Every 6 months
    b) Every year
    c) Every 2 years
    d) Every 5 years

657. As soon as you become self-employed you should register yourself for tax and National Insurance by ringing HM Revenue and Customs. Is this statement true or false?
    a) True
    b) False

658. Self-employed people have to keep detailed records of what they earn and spend on business because
    a) They have to submit their accounts to their banks every year.
    b) They have to submit their accounts to HM Revenue and Customs every year.

659. When do self-employed people have to inform the HM Revenue and Customs about their existence?
    a) As soon as they become self-employed.
    b) Within 2 Years of becoming self-employed.

660. What does Business Link do?
    a) Provide advice on becoming self employed.
    b) Link business together.

661. British citizens can work in any country that is a member of the European Economic Area (EEA). Is this statement true or false?
    a) True
    b) False

662. Women who are expecting a baby have a legal right to time off work for antenatal care. Is this statement true or false?
   a) True
   b) False

663. Pregnant women are entitled to at least 36 weeks' maternity leave. Is this statement true or false?
   a) True
   b) False

664. Only women who work full-time are entitled to maternity leave. Is this statement true or false?
   a) True
   b) False

665. Whether a woman is entitled to maternity pay depends on how long she has been working for that employer. Is this statement true or false?
   a) True
   b) False

666. How many weeks of maternity leave are all women entitled to?
   a) 16 weeks
   b) 26 weeks
   c) 30 weeks
   d) 36 weeks

667. How many weeks of paternity leave are fathers entitled to?
   a) 1 week
   b) 2 weeks
   c) 3 weeks
   d) 4 weeks

668. Fathers who have worked for their employer for at least 26 weeks are entitled to paternity leave. Is this statement true or false?
   a) True
   b) False

669. Where can you get advice on maternity and paternity matters?
   a) Your trade union representative
   b) Citizen Advice Bureau website
   c) Your personal officer at work
   d) All of the above

670. Where can you find advice about kinds of childcare facilities available and registered childminders in your area?
   a) From Citizen Advice Bureau
   b) From the Childcare Link website

671. The earliest legal age for children to do paid work is set at
   a) 10
   b) 12
   c) 14
   d) 16

672. With a licence from the local authority, children under the age of 14 can do the following specific work in (Select 3)
   a) Performing
   b) Modelling
   c) Sport
   d) Building

673. By Law, children aged 14 to 16 can only do
   a) Hard work
   b) Light work

674. Which of the job listed below are, children aged 14 to 16, not allowed to do? (Select 3 answers)
   a) Milk delivery
   b) Newspaper delivery
   c) Selling alcohol, cigarettes or medicines
   d) Working in a chip shop

675. When do children between the ages 14 to 16 have to get an employment card from their local authority and a medical certificate of fitness to work?
   a) When they apply for job in a newsagent.
   b) When they are doing any kind of work that might cause them injury.

676. Which these statements are true about working hours of children?
   a) They cannot work after 7 a.m. or before 7.p.m.
   b) They cannot work more than 2 hours on any school day or a Sunday

677. Which these statements are true about working hours of children?
   a) They can not work more than 16 hours in any school week.
   b) They cannot work for more than 1 hour before school start.

678. Who is responsible for checking whether children are employed legally?
    a) The local authority
    b) The Metropolitan Police Authority

679. Which exams are taken at 16?
    a) SATs
    b) A Levels
    c) Key Stage Tests
    d) GCSEs

680. The sight test is free for all people who are over 60. Is this statement true or false?
    a) True
    b) False

681. In most households in the UK women still have the most responsibility for child care and house work. Is this statement true or false?
    a) True
    b) False

682. In which year did Euro come into existence?
    a) 2000
    b) 2002
    c) 2004
    d) 2005

683. Prince of Wales is the current heir to the thrown. Is this statement true or false?
    a) True
    b) False

684. Over the last 20 years general population in the UK has
    a) Increased
    b) Decreased
    c) Remained the same

685. Apart from London, where else can you find large ethnic minority populations
    a) West Midlands
    b) South East of England
    c) South West of England
    d) Yorkshire and Humberside

686. Prescriptions are free for anyone who is 16 years or under. Is this statement true or false?
a) True
b) False

687. In Wales people under 25 or over 60 can get free dental treatment. Is this statement true or false?
a) True
b) False

688. At what age can you start to drive a car?
a) 16
b) 17
c) 18
d) 19

689. In England, a newly qualified driver must display an R-Plate for one year after passing the test. Is this statement true or false?
a) True
b) False

690. If your driving licence is from a country in the European Union (EU), how long can you drive with that licence in the UK?
a) 6 months
b) 12 months
c) 2 years
d) As long as your licence is valid.

691. When did the Second World War end?
a) 1918
b) 1939
c) 1945
d) 1950

692. Despite the laws that exist to prevent discrimination against women, they still do not always have the same access to promotion and better paid jobs. Is this statement true or false?
a) True
b) False

693. Currently one is three young people go on to higher education, but what is the government target?
   a) More than half
   b) More than three quarters
   c) More than 80%
   d) More than 90%

694. Secondary schools are smaller than primary schools. Is this statement true or false?
   a) True
   b) False

695. What are faith schools?
   a) Where they teach religion only.
   b) They are linked to certain faith.

696. In further education colleges, most courses are free up to the age of 19. Is this statement true or false?
   a) True
   b) False

697. When someone wants to drive your car, it is your responsibility to make sure they are insured to drive it.
   a) True
   b) False

698. When applying for a job, who can act as your referee? (Select 2 answers)
   a) Personal friend
   b) Current or previous employer
   c) Family member
   d) College tutor

699. Almost all the law protecting people at work apply equally to people doing part-time or full-time jobs. Is this statement true or false?
   a) True
   b) False

700. You have to take your complaint about unfair dismissal to Employment Tribunal within 3 months. Is this statement true or false?
   a) True
   b) False

Glossary

This glossary will help readers to understand the meanings of key words and key expressions in the ways in which they are used and the contexts in which they appear this handbook.

Some words or expressions in the definitions are written in bold. This can mean any of the following:

They are explained in another part of the glossary

They share the same kind of meaning as a word that is being defined but are used in another way in a sentence

They relate to the word that is being defined in some way, e.g. they have an exact opposite meaning or a very similar one-in this case, the word/s will be bracketed and preceded by 'see', e.g. (see vocational courses).

When words may be difficult to understand, an example of use may follow the definition.

The word that is bracketed after an entry relates to the particular context in which the word is being defined, e.g. applicant (employment).

A slash/separates different definition.

The convention s/he is used to mean 'she or he'.

absent from work	not at work, e.g. because of illness
abusive	unkind or violent-usually used to describe behaviour towards another person
academic course	a series of lessons in which a student learns by studying information that s/he reads in books (see **vocational course**)
access (internet)	connect to/connection

accountant		a person, whose job is to keep business records, to work out how much money a person or business is making or losing, and how much business tax needs to be paid (see **business accounts**)
AD		Anno Domini-referring to the number of years after Christ was born-used as a time reference, e.g. the Romans left Britain in 410 AD (see **BC**)
addictive substance		usually a type of drug that a person feels a strong need to take very often, and finds very difficult to stop using
adultery		sex between a married person and someone who is not their husband or Wife
afford		have enough money to pay for something
allegiance		loyalty to something, e.g. to a leader, a faith, a country or a cultural tradition
amphetamine		a type of drug which is addictive, powerful and illegal (see **addictive substances**)
annexation		taking control of a neighbouring country, usually by force
anonymous information		Information which is given by someone whose name is unknown
ante-natal care		medical care given to a woman (and to her unborn baby) while she is pregnant
applicant (employment)		someone who has asked an employer to give them a particular job-people often apply for jobs by writing a letter or completing a form
application letter		a formal letter sent to an employer asking for (applying for) a job
appoint		choose someone to do a job and formally offer it to them

arbitrary (law)		not bound by rules or law, and sometimes thought to be unfair
aristocracy		a group of people who are born into the highest class in society and who are traditionally very rich-a member of the aristocracy is called an aristocrat
armed forces		the army, navy and air force which defend a country in times of peace and war
arrested (police)		taken by the police to a police station and made to stay there to answer questions about illegal actions or activity (see **detained by the police**)
assault		the criminal act of using physical force against someone or of attacking someone, e.g. hitting someone
assessment methods (education)		ways to measure a student's abilities or skills, e.g. a teacher can assess a child's reading and writing skills using a variety of different methods
asylum		a place where people, who are accused of crime in another country, can live in safety
asylum seekers		people who leave their own country because they feel it is too dangerous for them to stay there (usually because of political reasons) and who then formally ask to stay in another country where it will be safer for them to live (see **refugees**)
ban		officially forbid
Bank Holiday		a day when most people have an official day off work and when banks and most other businesses are closed-a Bank Holiday can also be called a public holiday
baron		a man who is a member of the lower ranks of British nobility

BC		Before Christ-referring to the number of years before Christ was born-used as a time reference, e.g. 750 BC (see **AD**)
betting shop		a place where a person can go and pay to try to win money by gambling on the results of horse racing, football matches etc.
bid (money)		offer to pay a price for something when the cost is not fixed-other interested buyers may join in the bidding and the item will be sold to the highest bidder (the person who makes the highest offer)
binding, legally		an agreement to do something which, by law, cannot be changed or be withdrawn from
birth certificate		an official document that states the name of a person, the place and date of his/her birth, and the names and occupations of his/her parents
birth parent		a mother or father who is the natural, biological parent of a child
birth rate		the number of babies born, expressed as a percentage of a population, in a particular year or place
bishop		a senior priest in a Christian religion who is the head of different churches in a specified area
boom		a sharp rise in something-very often in business activity
bound, legally		obliged to do something in a way that follows certain laws
breach of contract		a situation arising when a person breaks a legal agreement to do or not to do something

British Empire		a large number of states under British colonial rule and which, at one time in history, accounted for one-quarter of the world's population. Many of these states are now independent, the rest are collectively known as the Commonwealth of Nations
broker (finance)		a person whose job is to give advice and to help select the most suitable and best value service in areas such as insurance and mortgages, also called a financial adviser
brutality		behaviour towards another person that is cruel and violent and causes harm
building society		a kind of bank which can be used for saving money or for borrowing money from in order to buy a house (see **mortgage**)
built-up area		a place where there are a lot of buildings and not many open spaces and where a lot of people live and/or work
bureaux de change		places where people can exchange one currency for another, e.g. they can sell pounds to buy euros
burglary		the criminal act of entering and stealing something from a building (see **theft**)
bursary		money in the form of a grant that a university gives to a student so they can study at university
business accounts		an official record of the amount of money a business is making, and how much it is paying for services or equipment etc, that is used to calculate the amount of tax that must be paid to the government (see **accountant**)
by-election		election which is held when an MP resigns or dies and when a new MP needs to be elected to replace him/her in Parliament before the next general election

cabinet (government)	a group of senior ministers who are responsible for controlling government policy
cable company	a company that can supply customers with a telephone or cable television connection
cannabis	an illegal drug that is usually smoked
captivity	being held in prison, not being allowed to move freely
carriageway	a single carriageway is a road which is only wide enough for one lane of traffic and which is divided from another road which takes traffic going in the opposite direction
a dual carriageway	is a road which is wide enough for two lanes of traffic and which is divided from another road which takes traffic in the opposite direction
cast a vote (government)	formally register one choice from a number of options so that a group decision can be made about the most popular outcome, e.g. so that the MP with the largest number of supporters is the one who is elected
casualties (medical)	people who are wounded, e.g. in an accident or in war
caution (employment, law)	a formal warning about something
cautious	careful, not wanting to get into a dangerous situation
census (government)	an official count of the number of people who live in a country and possibly including information about those people, e.g. age, race, marital status etc.
charity, give to	give money or take action to help people who are suffering from poverty, illnesses, starvation etc.

charter (government)		an official written statement which describes the rights and responsibilities of a state and its citizens
chieftain		ruler or leader of a clan in Scotland
child minder		a person whose job is to look after young children, usually while the children's parents are at work-a childminder usually has a qualification to do this kind of work
circulate (money)		pass from one person to another and then to another etc.
civil disobedience		the refusal of members of the public to obey laws, often because they want to protest against political issues
civil law		the legal system that deals with disputes between people or groups of people, e.g. domestic arguments, divorce, problems between landlords and tenants
civil service		the departments within government which manage the business of running the country-people who work for the government can be called civil servants
clamp (transport, police)		a metal device that is put on the wheel of a car to prevent it from being driven away (usually used because the car is parked somewhere illegally)-the driver will have to pay to have the damp removed
clan		a group of people or families who live under the rule of a chieftain and who are sometimes descendants of the same ancestor-this is a term traditionally used in Scotland
clarification (language)		a clear way of saying something that is easy to understand

clergy		Christian church officials, e.g. priests and bishops
coalition		a partnership between different political parties
cocaine		a type of drug which is addictive, powerful and illegal. It can be used by doctors to control pain (see **addictive substances**)
code of practice		an agreed set of professional rules and procedures that someone in work is expected to follow
colleagues		people that work together in the same company and who often have professional jobs
colonise		inhabit and take control of another country for the wealth and benefit of the home country-the people who move in and take control are called colonists
commemorate		do something to show that something or someone important is remembered, usually on a particular day
commit a crime		do something which is against the law (see **criminal, criminal offence**)
Commonwealth of Nations		an association of Britain and of sovereign states that used to be British colonies or states that are still ruled by Britain-the British monarch is accepted by the Commonwealth countries as their ruler
community events		events which are organised within a local area to help, in some way, the people who live or work in the same area, e.g. a town might hold a community event in order to raise money to buy special equipment for a local school

compensation (money)		money which must be paid to someone because they have suffered in some way, e.g. loss, injury. Compensation can also be paid to a person if their employer has treated them unfairly or illegally
compulsory testing		tests which must be done by law
concern		worry about an important problem/a worrying thing
concession		a right which is given to someone to end an argument or disagreement
condemn to death		a situation where a criminal is found guilty of such a serious crime that the judge decides to give the most severe punishment possible, which is death-this does not happen in the UK
confidential		information that is private and secret and only known to the giver and receiver of that information
confiscate (law) information		legally take possessions or property from the person who owns them
conquered		beaten in battle
consecutive		following one another without a break or interruption, e.g. next week we must have meetings on two consecutive days, Tuesday and Wednesday
constituency		a specific area where the voters who live in that place (its constituents) can elect an MP to represent them in Parliament
constitution (law)		the legal structure of established laws and principles which is used to govern a country
consumer problems		problems which people have that are to do with things that they have bought or services that they have paid for

181

contraception		methods used to prevent women who have sex from becoming pregnant, e.g. taking contraceptive pills, using a condom
contributions (finance)		money paid regularly by someone which will help pay for something which is worth much more, e.g. a pension
convention (government)		an official agreement, usually between countries, about particular rules or codes of behaviour
corrupt (behaviour)		acting in a dishonest and illegal way
coverage (media)		newspaper reports that can be read in the press (see **free press**)
credit card		a card which a person can use to buy goods or services which are paid for by a credit company- the credit company then sends the card-holder a monthly bill-goods can therefore be bought, but paid for later (see **debit card**)
criminal		a person who is found guilty of breaking the law
criminal offence		an illegal activity, e.g. burglary, for which the criminal may be prosecuted
Crusades		wars fought to try to spread Christianity
currency (money)		a particular system of money that a country or group of countries use, e.g. in the EU, the form of currency that is used most widely is the Euro
cut off (service)		disconnect the supply of something
debate		a discussion in which people give different opinions about something/to discuss and give different opinions about something

debit card	a card which a person can use to buy goods or services with money that is in their bank or building society account-the money is taken from their account automatically (see **credit card**)
decline in number	reduce, decrease, fall, go down
decree (law)	official order, law or decision
defeat	to be stronger than an opponent and therefore win a battle, a war, a competition etc.
defer	delay until a later time
degrading (treatment)	treatment that causes humiliation (see **humiliated**)
democratic country	a country which is governed by people who are elected by the population to represent them in Parliament
deport	make someone leave a country and, usually, return to the country from which they originally came-this is because the person who must be deported does not have the legal right to stay
deposit (housing)	an amount of money paid to a landlord when a person rents a flat or house-this money is given back when the person leaves, but only if the property or furniture has not been damaged
deposit (money)	an amount of money that is only part of the full price of something-the rest, 'the balance', must be paid later
descent, of	coming originally from, e.g. of Indian descent means being a member of a family coming originally from India (see **roots, ethnic origin**)
desert someone (law)	leave someone and not come back to help or look after them, e.g. to leave a husband or wife

detained by the police		kept at a police station and not allowed to leave (see **arrested**)
detect crimes (police)		discover and find out information about illegal actions or activities
devolution		the passing of power from a central government to another group at a regional or local level which can then be called a devolved administration
dialect		a form of a language which is spoken only by a particular social group or by a group of people living in a particular area
direct debit		an arrangement that a person makes to transfer an amount of money from his/her bank account into another account on a regular basis (see **standing order**)
disability, physical / mental		a condition that a person has that makes doing ordinary things like walking, seeing, speaking, talking, or learning difficult
discrimination		the act of treating an individual or a particular group of people in a way which is unfair, for example because of their race, nationality, sex, sexuality, age, or disability. Paying a woman less than a man for the same work is an example of discrimination
dismissal (employment)		removal from a job, the 'sack'
disputes		arguments or disagreements that are serious and about which people may take legal advice or action
disturbance (law)		a situation where people act in a loud or violent way and which upsets or disturbs other people, e.g. fighting in a public place

divorce		the legal end of a marriage/the act of ending a marriage
domestic policies		political decisions that relate to what is happening within a country (as opposed to in another country)
domestic rates		a type of tax in Northern Ireland which is paid by residents to their local authority and which helps to pay for local services, e.g. education, road repairs, policing, refuse collection
domestic violence		fighting or acting aggressively in the home and causing mental or physical harm to someone in the family
dominion		a country which was once colonised but that is now self-governing
dump		get rid of something, throw away-often in a place where rubbish should not be left/a place where rubbish is left in an untidy and unhealthy way
dwelling		a place where people live, e.g. a house, a flat
dynasty		a situation in which power is transferred from one member of a family to another and another over a long period of time, e.g. a son becomes King after his father before him and his grandfather before that
ecstasy		a type of drug which is illegal and dangerous. It makes users feel that they have lots of energy but can cause death (see **addictive substances**)
elect a person		choose someone by voting for them
electoral register		the official list of all the people in a country who are allowed to vote in an election
electorate		all the people who are allowed to vote in an election

eligible		allowed by law
emergency services		services that can be telephoned and that will come to the help of people when they need it quickly and very urgently, e.g. the police service, the fire service, the ambulance service, the coastguard service and, at sea, the lifeguard service
employ		give someone work and pay them to do it
employee		someone who is paid by an employer to do a job
employer		a person or company that gives work to other people and pays them for doing it
engagement (family)		an agreement between two people that they will get married at some time in the future-these people are engaged to one another but not married yet (see **fiancé and fiancée**)
enterprise (business)		business energy-the starting and running of business activities
entitled (law)		officially allowed (to do something)
entrepreneurial		prepared to take risks with money in order to start a business / prepared to take risks with money to make more money in business
ethnic minority		a group of people who are of a different race from the race of the majority of the population in a particular country
ethnic origin		the country of birth, someone's race or the nationality of someone when they were born / the customs and place from which a person and their family originated (see **roots**)
European Union (or EU)		a political and economical association of European countries which encourages trade and cooperation between its member states

evict (housing)		order someone legally to leave the house where they are living
evidence, collecting		looking for and getting information, documents or items that show for certain that something has happened, e.g. the police went to the criminal's house to collect as much evidence as possible (see **proof**)
exchange rate		the amount of money in one currency that you need to buy a certain amount of money in another currency, e.g. £ 1 = $1.9 (see bureaux de change). The exchange rate can vary from day to day
executed		killed as an act of punishment
exiled		sent to another country and not allowed to return as an act of political punishment
expel		force someone officially to leave an organisation of some kind
exploitation		a situation in which someone is made to do something unfairly because they are given nothing or very little for doing it, e.g. the women were exploited by their employer who paid them less than the minimum wage and also forced them to work overtime
expression, freedom of		talking about personal ideas or beliefs without getting into any legal trouble for doing so
facilities in the community		local services that the public can use, e.g. libraries, schools, hospitals
false statement (police)		a report that contains untruthful information, e.g. lies told in answer to police questions
famine		a situation in which there is very little food for a long time and people often die because of this

fiancé		a man who has formally agreed to marry a woman
fiancée		a woman who has formally agreed to marry a man (see **engagement**)
fine (law)		an amount of money that a person must pay because they have broken the law (see **on-the-spot-fines, penalty**)
firearm		any kind of gun
first past the post		a system of election in which the candidate with the largest number of votes in a particular constituency wins a seat in Parliament
flooding (housing)		water coming inside a property (and which probably causes damage to it)
forced labour		work which is usually physical and which workers have to do, but do not want to do
free press		newspapers and other reporting media that are not controlled by government and can therefore write freely, without restriction, about anything they think their readers will be interested in
gambling (money)		risking money to try to win more money, e.g. in card games or by trying to guess the winner of a horse race or football match
gap year (education)		a year between leaving school and going to university during which many students choose to gain experience through travelling, or to earn money by taking a job
general election		a situation in which all the citizens of a country who are allowed to vote choose the people they wish to represent them in their government-in Britain this usually happens every five years (see **MP**)

government policies		official ideas and beliefs that are agreed by a political party about how to govern the country (see **party politics**)
grant (money)		an amount of money paid by an authority to help a person or organisation pay for a particular thing, e.g. an education course, a business expansion
guerrilla war		a war in which several small groups of people fight against an opposition
guidance (law)		advice about how or where to get help
guilty (law)		found by a court to have committed a crime (see **innocent**)
hard drugs		drugs which are illegal and are very powerful and addictive
harassment (behaviour)		rude, offensive, threatening or bullying behaviour-a word often used to describe this kind of behaviour in a workplace
health authority, local		an organisation which manages health care and from which people can get advice about where to find medical help
health hazards		things that might be dangerous to someone's health, e.g. smoking is a hazard to health because it can cause lung cancer
hearing, in court		a meeting in court when a judge hears information about a crime that has been committed
heir		someone who will legally receive another person's money, property, possessions or position when that person dies
helmet		a hard hat that protects the head against injury-a crash helmet must be worn by someone who is riding a motorcycle

heroin		a type of drug which is addictive, powerful and illegal (see **addictive substance**)
higher education		education that students receive at college or university
holding public office		having a job in one of the services or industries that are managed by the government
Holy Land		the area in the Middle East in and around Jerusalem where all the biblical events took place
House of Commons		that part of the Houses of Parliament where MPs who are elected by the voting public debate political issues
House of Lords		that part of the Houses of Parliament where the people who have inherited seats or been especially chosen by the Prime Minister debate political issues
Houses of Parliament		the building in London which comprises the House of Commons, the House of Lords and other offices where the British Parliament meets, debates and passes laws
household		the home and the people who live in it/ something that relates to the home, e.g. household chores are jobs that need to be done in the home like cleaning and cooking
humiliated		feel ashamed, stupid or embarrassed because of something that happens to you, usually when other people are there
immigration		enter another country to live and work there- someone who does this is an immigrant (see **migrate**)
inappropriate touching		touching someone on a part of his/her body or in a way that is offensive and not acceptable in a particular situation

indecent remarks		something that is said that contains words which are rude, sexual and offensive
independents (politics)		MPs who do not represent any of the main political parties
inflation (money)		the rate at which prices rise over a period of time
infrastructure		structured network that is necessary for the successful operation of a business or transport system, e.g. roads or railways
inheritance		a sum of money, possessions or property that someone has the legal right to receive after the death of (usually) a relative, e.g. a son might inherit his father's fortune
inhuman (behaviour)		very harsh, cruel and degrading
innocent (law)		found by a court NOT to be responsible for committing a crime (see **guilty**)
inpatient		someone who needs medical care and needs to stay in hospital overnight or longer
instalments (money)		a series of equal payments which are paid regularly over a period of time until the total cost of something is paid, e.g. a person may pay for a TV that costs £200 in ten monthly instalments of £20
insulting words		rude words which also make people feel very unhappy, worried or stupid
insure		pay money to an insurance company in case e.g. a car or property is damaged-if this happens, the insurance company will help to pay for repairs
intentionally		on purpose, deliberately

interest (money)		extra money that must be paid to a lender when someone borrows money-this is usually calculated as a percentage of the loan-if the interest rate is 10% and the person borrows £100, the interest that must be paid on the loan will be an extra £10
internet café		a place where people can go and pay to use a computer to look up information on websites or to send emails-the cost depends on how long they want to use a computer for, e.g. 30 minutes
interpreter		a person whose job is to change something that is spoken or written in one language into another language without changing the meaning
irretrievably broken down		when there is no hope of solving problems and making a bad situation better again
Islamic mortgage		a loan for buying a house, and when the person who receives the loan only needs to pay back the original sum-no extra money needs to be paid (see **interest**)
judge (law)		the most important official in court whose job is to make sure that court proceedings are lawful and fair, and to decide which punishment to give a criminal if s/he is found guilty by the court
judiciary		all the judges in a country who, together, are responsible for using the law of the land in the correct way
jury		ordinary people (usually a group of 12 people) who listen to information and then decide whether someone is guilty or innocent in a court of law
labour (employment)		work which is often physical / workers

landlord, landlady (housing)		a man (landlord) or woman (landlady) who owns a house or flat and rents it to people (tenants) who must pay them money (rent) to live there
landlord, landlady (pub)		the owner or manager of a pub
lane (transport)		part of a road, usually marked by white lines, which is only wide enough for one vehicle to travel in (see **carriageway**)
legal		allowed to do by law or must do by law
legal aid		money that a person can ask for to help them pay for the services of a solicitor and, if necessary, court costs
legal procedure		the way that something is done by law
legislative power		the power to make laws
legitimate children		children whose parents are married to each other when they are born
leisure centre		a building where people can go and pay to do sports indoors, e.g. swimming, badminton
letting agent		a service which helps landlords find tenants and tenants find places to rent (see **landlord, landlady**)
liberty		freedom
lock		close something securely, usually with a key, so that other people cannot easily open it
long-standing		having already existed for a long time
L-plates		a sign on a car to show that the driver is still learning to drive and has not yet passed their driving test-an L-plate is a red L in a white square

magistrate	a person who acts as a judge in a court case where the crime is not as serious as some others
mainland	an area of land which forms a country and does not include any of its surrounding islands
manufacturer	the maker of a product which is sold to the public
marital status	information about whether a person is single, married, separated or divorced that is often asked for on official forms
maternity leave	time allowed off work for a woman during her pregnancy and after her baby is born and during which time she usually continues to receive a wage (see **paternity leave**)
maternity services	medical and social help relating to motherhood from early pregnancy until after the baby has been born
media	all the organisations that give information to the public, e.g. newspapers, magazines, television, radio and the internet
mediation	advice and support given by a person or organisation to end an argument between two other people or groups of people who cannot agree about something
medical consultation	speaking to a doctor and getting information and advice, e.g. about health issues, illness
mental illness	an illness in which a person appears to behave or think in ways that are not considered to be normal, e.g. 'depression' is a mental illness that makes people feel unnecessarily sad, worried or frightened and can prevent them from doing routine things like shopping, having fun with friends etc.

meter (housing)		a machine that shows, in units or numbers, how much electricity, gas or water has been used in a household
meter reading (housing)		the number on a meter that shows how much electricity, gas or water has been used
migrate (people)		move to another country to live and work there-someone who does this is a migrant (see **immigration**)
military service, compulsory		every adult (usually male) must join the armed forces for a particular period of time-this is not required by law in the UK
minor offences		illegal actions or activities that are considered NOT to be very serious, e.g. theft of a very small amount of money (see **serious offences**)
mislead (law)		give wrong or incomplete or false information on purpose so that someone else is not told the truth
missionaries		people who travel to other countries to teach and spread a religious faith
misuse		use something in a wrong way or for a wrong reason
molestation		a sexual attack on someone (often a child)
monarch		the king or queen of a country
monopoly (business)		a power which has exclusive control over a supply of goods or over a service and where competitors are not allowed to deal in the same business
mortgage		a loan, usually from a building society or bank, that is used to buy or help buy a house or flat-the loan is usually paid back in instalments over a number of years (see **building society**)

motor (transport)		a machine that makes something move/a car
MP		Member of Parliament-the person who is elected by his or her constituents to represent them in government
national issues		political problems that can affect everyone who lives in a country
nationalised		bought and then controlled by central government-relating to an industry or service that was previously owned privately (see **privatise**)
naturalised citizen		someone who is born in one country but becomes a citizen of another country
nobility		the group of people in a country who belong to the highest social class-some of whom may have titles, e.g. Lord or Duke, (see **aristocracy**)
not-for-profit		a way of doing business in which an organisation or company will not try to make any money from providing their service or goods
notice, to give		to give someone information about something that is going to happen in the future that will change a situation
notice (employment)		a length of time that an employee must continue to work after telling an employer that s/he wants to leave the job/a length of time that an employer must continue to employ someone after asking her/him to leave, e.g. my boss only gave me one week's notice so I was really upset
nuisance (behaviour)		something that annoys or causes problems for other people
obstructive (behaviour)		being difficult, and stopping someone from doing something or stopping something from happening on purpose

occupy a country		invade a country and take control of it
occupation (employment)		job
offensive (behaviour)		rude and upsetting
office, to be in		to be in power in government
off-licence		a shop that sells alcohol in bottles or cans, e.g. wine, beer
Olympic team		a team of sportsmen and women who represent their country in the Olympics-an international athletics competition held every four years
online		on the internet
on-the-spot-fines		an immediate demand for money which must be paid as a punishment for doing something wrong, e.g. to receive an on-the-spot fine for driving too fast
Opposition		the second largest party that is not in power in the government, e.g. in 2006, the Labour Party was in power and the Conservatives were in Opposition and David Cameron was the Leader of the Opposition
outpatient		someone who needs medical care in a hospital but does not need to stay overnight
packaging		material, e.g. boxes, see-through plastic, that covers and protects things that are for sale, e.g. food
padlock		a small lock which can be used to keep things safe and secure by stopping anyone else opening or stealing them
party politics		the shared and particular ideas and beliefs of an organised group of politicians, e.g. the Labour Party

paternity leave		time allowed off work for a man whose wife or partner is going to have a baby or has just had a baby and during which time he usually continues to receive a wage (see **maternity leave**)
patient (medical)		someone whom a doctor looks after or who needs medical care because they are ill, have an injury etc.
patriarchy		a system of society in which men hold all the power and in which power can be passed from father to son
patriotism		the pride of belonging to, and love of, a country
Patron Saint		a Christian Saint who, according to religious belief, protects a particular place or a particular group of people
Peers		members of the House of Lords
penalty (law)		punishment for breaking the law, e.g. a fine (see **on-the-spot fines**)
pension plan, pay into a		to save money regularly while a person is working so that when a person stops going to work at 60 or older, there will be enough money to provide him/her with a pension (see **State pension**)
performing (theatre)		acting or dancing
perishable food		food which can go bad and become uneatable quite quickly, e.g. fresh meat and fish, milk
permit (law)		a document that allows someone to legally do something, e.g. a work permit
persecuted		hunted and punished, perhaps even killed, e.g. someone might be persecuted for holding a particular religious belief

personal details		information about a person that can be used to identify them, e.g. their name, date of birth, address, marital status etc
personnel officer		someone whose job in a company is to employ staff and to help solve problems that employees have at work
phonecard, pre-paid		a card that can be bought and then used to make a certain number of phone calls up to the value of the card
PIN number		four numbers which have to be tapped into a cash machine if someone wants to withdraw money from their account or pay for something using credit or debit cards. Using a personal identification number (PIN) stops other people from using cards if they are stolen so the numbers must be remembered and kept secret
places of worship		religious buildings like churches or mosques where people can go to practise their religion, e.g. to pray or sing
plague (medical)		a disease that people easily catch from one another and from which many people die at a particular time in history
pluralistic society		a society in which the population is multi-racial, multi-religious and has many different political ideas
pocket money		a small amount of money that a parent might give to his/her child on a regular basis, e.g. once a week, so that the child can buy his/her own comics or sweets etc
pogroms		the intentional killing of many people usually because of their race or religious belief
pooled savings		amounts of money that have been saved by different people and added together to make a larger sum of jointly-owned money

Pope, the		the leader of the Roman Catholic Church
possessions		things that people own, e.g. a car, clothes, a television, books
practise a religion		actively live according to the rules, customs and beliefs of that religion, e.g. go to church, take part in prayer, wear special clothing etc
pregnancy		the nine-month period before birth during which a baby grows inside its mother-the mother is pregnant at this time
prehistoric		a time in history before any records were written down
prescription (medical)		a note from a doctor saying which medicines a patient needs
pressure group		a group of people who try to persuade the government to do something or to persuade the public to change their opinion about something
Prime Minister		the Member of Parliament who is the leader of the political party in power and therefore of the whole government
privatised		bought and then controlled by the private sector-relating to an industry or service that was previously owned by the government (see **nationalised**)
process of precedent		a system in which previous actions or decisions influence and support future actions or decisions (often in legal judgements)
prohibit		say that something is illegal/stop someone doing something/ make something illegal or forbid something

promotion (employment)	movement to a better or to a more important job within the same company, e.g. she was promoted from shop assistant to sales manageress
proof	information, items, documents etc. that show that something has definitely happened (see **evidence**)
proportional representation	a system of election in which political parties are allowed a number of seats in Parliament that represents their share of the total number of votes cast
prosperity	a time of wealth or increase in fortune
provinces	areas into which a country is divided for governmental reasons
pub	public house-a place where adults over the age of 18 can buy and drink alcohol
public, a member of the	an person who is an ordinary member of the community and not a government official
public body	a governmental department or a group of people who represent or work for the government and work for the good of the general public
public order (law)	a situation where rules are obeyed in a public place
public place	a place which is not private and where ordinary people can spend time together, or on their own, e.g. a cinema, a restaurant, a library, a pub, a park
punctual	arriving at the right time, not being late for something, e.g. work or a doctor's appointment
racial	relating to race, e.g. racial discrimination (see **discrimination**)

racially motivated crime	a crime that is committed against someone because of their race or ethnic origin
racism	aggressive behaviour towards (or treatment of) people who come from a different race by people who wish to be unkind and unfair to them
raising (family)	looking after children as they grow so that they are safe and healthy
rape	the criminal act of a person forcing another person to have sex, often involving violence
receipt (money) (employment)	a piece of paper with a description of something that has been bought and its price-given by a shop to a customer as a record of the purchase
recruit	find people and offer them work in a company or business
recycle rubbish	separate rubbish into different materials, e.g. put all the paper in one place and all the glass in another, so that each material can be processed in a separate way and used again, e.g. broken glass can be made into new bottles
redundant (employment)	no longer needed to do a particular job, e.g. if a person is made redundant, there is no longer a job for that person to do in a particular company and they will be asked to leave-if this happens the employee may be entitled to receive an amount of money (redundancy pay)
referendum	a vote by the public or by a governing body to decide on a course of action or to make a political decision
Reformation, the	the religious movement in the 16th century that challenged the authority of the Pope and established Protestant churches in Europe-Protestant comes from the word 'protest'

refuge		a place where a person can stay and be kept safe from danger
refugees		people who must leave the country where they live, often because of war or political reasons (see **asylum seekers**)
refund (money)		give a customer an amount of money back that is equal to the price of something s/he bought but returned to the shop, e.g. because the item does not work properly
remain silent (police)		say nothing, not to answer questions
rent (housing)		pay to live in a room, flat or house that is owned by someone else
report a crime		tell the police about an illegal action or activity
residence		the place where someone lives, their address
residential trips (school)		visits to places when students stay away from home for one night or longer and have to sleep in other accommodation
resign (employment)		decide officially to leave a certain job
restrict (immigration)		control and/or limit the number of people, e.g. a government might restrict the number of immigrants who can come and live in a country
retail work		jobs that involve working in shops and selling goods to customers
retire (employment)		stop going to work, usually at the age of 65 or older
rise (in number, price)		increase, go up

rival viewpoints		opinions that are held by different people or groups of people that are in opposition to each other
roots (family)		the place that someone relates to because that was where s/he was born or where his/her family had their established home
scratch card		a card that a person buys and then rubs with a coin to see if they have won money (see **gambling**)
scrutinise		examine all the details
seat (government)		a position that is officially held by someone in government who has been elected by the public and authorised to represent them
second hand goods		something that someone else has already owned
security		protection from something that could be dangerous, e.g. a person or thing that is secure is safe and protected from danger
self employed person		someone who works for themselves and not for an employer
sentence (law)		length of time a criminal must stay in prison as a punishment for the crime s/he has committed-this is decided by a judge at the end of a court case
separation (family)		a situation where a married couple no longer live together but are not yet divorced
serious misconduct (employment)		behaviour by someone in a job which is dishonest, bad or unprofessional, and because of which they may lose their job
serious offences (law)		illegal actions or activities which are very bad and for which someone may have to go to prison for a long time, e.g. rape, murder (see **minor offences**)

Shadow Cabinet	a group of senior MPs with special responsibilities who belong to a party that is not in government (which can also be called the Opposition)
Sheriff (law)	a judge in Scotland
sick pay	money received by an employee when s/he is unable to work because of illness
signatory	a person who signs their name (puts their signature) on an official document-e.g, to show their agreement to an official arrangement
slavery	a system in which people bought and owned other people (slaves) who were then forced to work for nothing in return (see **forced labour**)
solicitor	a professional person whose job is to give legal advice and prepare documents for legal procedures, e.g. divorce, buying and selling houses
Speaker, the	the person in government who controls the way issues are debated in Parliament
stand for office	apply to be elected as an MP or local councillor
standing order	an arrangement in which a bank or building society takes a fixed amount of money from one account and pays it into another account on a regular basis (see **direct debit**)
start-up loans	money given to someone to start up a new business that must be paid back with interest later (see **grant, interest**)
State pension	money paid regularly by the government to people who have retired from work, usually when they are 65 or older

stepfamily	a family in which the mother or father is not the biological parent of one or more of the children, e.g. when a divorced woman re-marries, her new husband will be the stepfather to the children from her previous marriage
strike, to go on	refuse to work in order to protest against something, e.g. low wages, long hours
subscribe to a magazine	pay enough money so that copies of a magazine can be sent to an address at regular intervals over a period of time (usually for a year)
successor (government)	a person who comes after another and who will often receive some kind of power when that happens, e.g. a son who becomes king when his father, the old king, dies is the successor to the throne
surveyor (housing)	a person who examines a property (usually when it is for sale) and checks the condition of the building. S/he then writes an official report (a survey) which gives important information to the buyer about any problems, or about any repairs that might need to be done
suspect (crime)	a person who police think may be guilty of a committing a crime, but this is not certain yet
suspend	to officially stop, usually for a short time, something from happening or operating
taster session (training)	an introductory part of a course that allows someone to try it and to see if it is what they would like to do
tenancy	the period of time that a tenant rents a property from a landlord or landlady-often also relating to conditions about renting the property

tenant		a person who pays money to a landlord to live in rented accommodation-a flat or a house
terrorism		violence used by people who want to force governments to do something-the violence is usually random and unexpected so no one can feel really safe from it
theft		the criminal act of stealing something from a person, building or place (see **burglary**)
therapist (psychology)		a professional person whose job is to help people to understand why they have problems and to help them solve their problems
timescale		the planned length of time it takes to complete something, usually at work
toddler (family)		small child, usually 1-2 years old-the age at which small children learn to walk
torture		hurt someone in a very cruel way and on purpose, e.g. to try to make them give information or to punish them
tow away a car		remove a car from a place-another vehicle pulls it along-usually because it has been illegally parked
trade union		an association of workers that protects its members political rights
trader		someone who trades-who buys and sells goods
treaty		an official written agreement between countries or governments
tried in front of a judge		facts of the case heard and the sentence decided in an official court of law
tuition fees		money paid to a teacher or to a school for being taught something

unemployed		not doing a job and not getting any wages
uprising		a violent revolt or rebellion against an authority
utilities, public		services that the public can use, e.g. the supply of water, gas or electricity
vacancy (employment)		a job that is available and that an employer needs someone to do
valid		legally acceptable, e.g. when someone wants to enter another country his/her passport must be valid for that to be allowed
vehicle (transport)		something in which people can travel on the roads, e.g. a car or bus
vetoed, to be vetoed		officially refused permission to do something, often by an organisation
victim		someone who is hurt or harmed by something that another person has done
vocational course		a series of lessons in which a student is taught the practical skills that are necessary to do a certain job, e.g. to become a plumber or car mechanic (see **academic course**)
volt		a measurement of electrical force
voluntarily		in a willing way, e.g. a person who does something voluntarily does it because they want to, and not because someone has asked them to do it or because someone has said that they must do it
voluntary work		work which someone does because they want to and which they do for free, i.e. they do not receive any payment (see **volunteer**)
volunteer		someone who works for free or who offers to do something without payment (see **voluntary work**)

vulnerable people		people who can be easily hurt or harmed e.g. because of their age
wages (pay)		an amount of money paid for work
war effort		the work that people did in order to support the country in whatever way they could during wartime.
welfare benefits		amounts of money paid by the government to people who have very little money of their own and who are perhaps unable to work or elderly or sick or disabled etc.
will (law)		a legal document that gives instructions about what a person wants to happen when s/he dies, e.g. about who should have their property, money or possessions
withdraw (law)		step back from and stop taking part in a formal arrangement or activity
withdraw (money)		take money out of an bank account or cash machine
workforce		the group of people who work for a particular company or business or, on a larger scale, all the people who can work in a particular country or part of the world etc.
working days		the days on which, typically, most people go to work-in the UK these are Monday, Tuesday, Wednesday, Thursday and Friday
Yellow Pages		a book that lists names, addresses and telephone numbers of businesses, services and organisations in an area

Answers

1	c	34.	b	67.	b	100.	c	133.	d
2.	b,c	35.	b	68.	a,b,c	101.	c	134.	a,b,d
3.	b	36.	a	69.	a	102.	b	135.	b
4.	b	37.	b	70.	d	103.	a	136.	c
5.	c	38.	b	71.	a	104.	d	137.	a
6.	a	39.	a	72.	c	105.	b	138.	d
7.	d	40.	b	73.	a	106.	c	139.	b
8.	a	41.	a	74.	a	107.	a	140.	b
9.	b	42.	a	75.	b	108.	b	141.	b
10.	d	43.	b	76.	b	109.	d	142.	a
11.	b	44.	a	77.	a	110.	c	143.	d
12.	c	45.	d	78.	b	111.	c	144.	c
13.	c	46.	c	79.	c	112.	b	145.	d
14.	d	47.	b	80.	d	113.	b	146.	d
15.	c	48.	b	81.	a	114.	c	147.	c
16.	c	49.	b	82.	b	115.	d	148.	b
17.	a	50.	a,b	83.	c	116.	a	149.	a
18.	b	51.	b	84.	d	117.	b	150.	d
19.	b	52.	c,d	85.	a	118.	c	151.	a
20.	c	53.	a	86.	b	119.	d	152.	b
21.	c	54.	b	87.	a,b,d	120.	a	153.	d
22.	b	55.	a	88.	b	121.	b	154.	a
23.	a	56.	b	89.	d	122.	a	155.	c
24.	a	57.	a	90.	d	123.	a	156.	a,c
25.	b	58.	c	91.	b	124.	a	157.	b
26.	b	59.	a	92.	d	125.	b	158.	a
27.	a	60.	d	93.	b,c	126.	a	159.	b,c
28.	a	61.	d	94.	b	127.	d	160.	a,b,d
29.	c	62.	a	95.	a	128.	b	161.	b
30.	c	63.	a	96.	b	129.	b	162.	b
31.	c	64.	b	97.	a	130.	a	163.	c
32.	b	65.	b	98.	a	131.	b	164.	a
33.	b	66.	a	99.	c	132.	d	165.	c

No.	Ans.	No.	Ans.	No.	Ans.	No.	Ans.	No.	Ans.
166.	a	202.	a	238.	c	274.	a	310.	b
167.	c	203.	b	239.	b,d	275.	b	311.	c
168.	a	204.	b	240.	c	276.	b	312.	b
169.	a	205.	c	241.	b	277.	a,b,d	313.	a,c
170.	c	206.	c	242.	a,c	278.	a	314.	a
171.	d	207.	c	243.	b	279.	c	315.	a
172.	a,b	208.	b	244.	b	280.	c	316.	c
173.	c	209.	d	245.	a	281.	a	317.	a
174.	b	210.	c	246.	c	282.	a,b,c	318.	a
175.	b	211.	b	247.	a	283.	a	319.	b
176.	c	212.	b	248.	b	284.	b	320.	b,c
177.	b	213.	a,b	249.	d	285.	a,b,d	321.	b
178.	c	214.	a	250.	a	286.	a	322.	b
179.	c	215.	a	251.	d	287.	c	323.	c
180.	c	216.	a	252.	b	288.	c	324.	b
181.	b	217.	b	253.	b	289.	b	325.	a
182.	d	218.	d	254.	b	290.	a,b,d	326.	c
183.	b	219.	a,b,d	255.	a	291.	a	327.	a,b,c
184.	a	220.	b,c	256.	a	292.	b	328.	b
185.	a,b	221.	b	257.	a	293.	a	329.	a,c
186.	a,b,d	222.	d	258.	c	294.	b	330.	b
187.	d	223.	a	259.	b,d	295.	a	331.	a
188.	b	224.	b	260.	b	296.	b,c	332.	b
189.	d	225.	b	261.	a	297.	a	333.	b,c
190.	c	226.	c	262.	b	298.	a	334.	a,b
191.	a	227.	b	263.	c	299.	b	335.	d
192.	c	228.	b	264.	a	300.	a,d	336.	c
193.	b	229.	c	265.	c	301.	a,c	337.	b
194.	a	230.	a,d	266.	a,d	302.	a	338.	b
195.	a	231.	b	267.	a	303.	a	339.	b
196.	a,b,c	232.	a	268.	a	304.	a	340.	a
197.	b	233.	a	269.	c	305.	b,d	341.	b
198.	c	234.	a	270.	c	306.	b	342.	a,c,d
199.	b	235.	a	271.	a,b,d	307.	b	343.	d
200.	b	236.	b	272.	b	308.	c	344.	a
201.	a	237.	b	273.	b	309.	b	345.	b

346. b	382. a	418. a,c	454. d	490. b
347. c	383. b	419. b	455. b	491. b
348. a	384. a	420. a,b,d	456. b	492. b
349. c	385. a	421. b	457. b	493. a
350. b	386. a,b,d	422. b	458. b	494. a
351. a,b	387. b	423. a	459. b	495. a,b
352. b	388. a,b,d	424. a	460. b	496. a
353. b	389. a	425. b	461. b	497. a
354. b	390. a	426. c	462. b	498. a
355. a	391. a	427. c	463. a	499. b
356. c	392. a	428. b	464. b	500. b
357. a	393. a	429. a,b	465. a	501. b
358. a	394. a	430. a,b,d	466. a	502. a
359. a,c	395. b	431. b	467. a	503. b
360. a	396. b	432. a	468. a,c,d	504. b
361. b	397. b	433. a,c	469. b	505. a
362. b	398. a	434. c	470. b,c	506. a
363. a	399. b	435. a,b,c	471. a,c,d	507. a,b,d
364. a	400. b	436. b	472. a,b	508. a
365. b	401. b	437. b,c	473. b,c	509. b
366. a	402. a	438. a	474. c,d	510. a
367. a	403. b	439. a,b	475. b	511. a
368. b	404. b	440. a	476. b	512. b
369. b	405. b	441. b	477. a	513. a,b,d
370. d	406. b	442. b	478. a	514. a
371. a	407. a	443. b	479. b	515. a
372. a	408. a,b,d	444. a,c,d	480. b	516. b
373. b	409. a,c,d	445. a,c	481. a,b,d	517. a,c
374. b,c,d	410. a,c	446. b	482. a,b,c	518. a,c
375. a,c,d	411. a	447. b	483. a,b,d	519. b
376. c	412. a	448. a	484. a	520. a
377. b	413. b	449. a	485. a	521. b
378. b	414. b	450. d	486. b	522. a
379. a	415. a,b,c	451. b	487. a	523. a
380. a	416. b	452. a	488. a	524. a
381. b	417. b	453. a,c	489. a,b,d	525. a

526.	a	562.	b	598.	a,b,c	634.	a	670.	b
527.	a,b,d	563.	d	599.	a	635.	a	671.	c
528.	b	564.	a	600.	b	636.	a	672.	a,b,c
529.	c	565.	b	601.	b	637.	b	673.	b
530.	a	566.	a,d	602.	c	638.	a,b,d	674.	a,c,d
531.	b	567.	d	603.	d	639.	b	675.	b
532.	a	568.	a	604.	a	640.	a	676.	b
533.	b	569.	d	605.	b	641.	a	677.	b
534.	a	570.	b	606.	a	642.	a	678.	a
535.	b	571.	a,b,d	607.	a	643.	b	679.	d
536.	b	572.	b	608.	b,c	644.	b	680.	a
537.	b	573.	a	609.	a,b	645.	d	681.	a
538.	a,b	574.	b	610.	b,c,d	646.	a,d	682.	b
539.	b	575.	a,c	611.	b	647.	b	683.	a
540.	a,b	576.	a	612.	b	648.	a	684.	a
541.	b	577.	b	613.	b	649.	b	685.	a,b,d
542.	b	578.	a	614.	a,b	650.	b,d	686.	a
543.	b	579.	b,c	615.	a,b,c	651.	a	687.	a
544.	b	580.	b	616.	b	652.	b	688.	b
545.	b	581.	d	617.	b	653.	a	689.	b
546.	a	582.	a,c	618.	b	654.	b	690.	d
547.	b	583.	a	619.	a	655.	a	691.	c
548.	a,b,d	584.	a	620.	a	656.	b	692.	a
549.	b	585.	a	621.	b	657.	a	693.	a
550.	c	586.	a	622.	a	658.	b	694.	b
551.	b,c,d	587.	a	623.	b	659.	a	695.	b
552.	b,d	588.	d	624.	a	660.	a	696.	a
553.	b	589.	a	625.	a	661.	a	697.	a
554.	b	590.	a	626.	b	662.	a	698.	b,d
555.	b	591.	a	627.	a,b,c	663.	b	699.	a
556.	a	592.	b	628.	a	664.	b	700.	a
557.	a	593.	a	629.	b	665.	a		
558.	b	594.	b	630.	a	666.	b		
559.	a,b,d	595.	a	631.	b	667.	b		
560.	b	596.	a,b,d	632.	a	668.	a		
561.	b	597.	b	633.	b,c,d	669.	d		